Mere Sense

A Memoir of Men, Migraine,
and the Mysteries of
Being Highly Sensitive

By Monica Nelson

www.authormonicanelson.com
www.meresense.com

This story is true from one person's perspective: mine. My version of events may or may not coincide with others I've written about –
we all know how different perspectives see events differently.
I spent many hours contemplating whether to use real names. I have chosen to use substitute first names with no last name designation in most cases; in others, only to identify the person generically. Every person mentioned here has played a vital part in my growth and movement toward healing.
They are angels of the most wonderful kind, and I thank each and every one of them in advance.

Find ecstasy in life; the mere sense of living is joy enough.
--Emily Dickinson

Table of Contents

Prologue

<u>What's Wrong with Me?</u>

"I'm sorry," I said barely above a whisper.

The words bit at my tongue as they tumbled out of my mouth. Horrified at my own audacity, I sent the handset back into its cradle before he had a chance to respond. I slid down the wall of my apartment and pushed hard against it, pounding the heels of my hands onto my forehead, and curled myself into a ball. *Stupid, stupid, stupid, what have I done,* streaked through my mind.

I knew it an inappropriate action before I did it. I barely knew him, and I'd called him at his girlfriend's house. And then I hung up. Like some inexperienced child, not the 20-year-old I was. It wasn't like me. I was typically the wallflower, preferring not to be seen. But the last couple of months had me fighting daily the desperation I felt.

The agony that drove my actions was sourced from so many directions; I could scarcely distinguish them. An emotional upheaval resulting in a lapse of expected behavior, a perplexing sense of who I really was, and the resulting pain of it all coming together in one moment. It was this pain from which I sought relief. After dropping my ill-fated apology, I felt no better. I had delivered the dismal dispatch in hopes of relieving overwhelming guilt. Fixing the wrong I'd committed. My failing having built in despair month-by-month, day-by-day, hour-by-hour, minute-by-minute, fueled by overheard gossip.

Humiliation growing from the moment I walked away from him months prior. The people who knew about it thought I was strange. Unpredictable. Worse, emotional. The e-word arising like a bomb in the thinly masked conversations fueling my infamy.

In the quiet of those awful minutes following my

blunder, I hugged my knees. Turning my head to the side, the clock ticked away exhausted moments. I sank further into myself. No lingering thought, simply an unspoken hatred for myself. A feeling, pushing outward from my bones and skin. The growing expression a sinister reminder of the person I barely knew but should know best.

As I sat on my kitchen floor, tears rolling down my face, I hit a new realization. Something had to change. I couldn't go on another day, another minute, without understanding and overcoming. This was it – my lowest point. I defiantly resolved to go no lower.

How I got here, and where I went from there is my story. I have changed many of the names in it. Only those folks can detail their journey through life. To get where I wanted to go, I had to focus on my reaction to mutual events. And what I could learn from our interaction. It is important to remember that this story details solely my memory and my interpretation of those events. I have made every attempt to speak the truth to the best of my ability.

Chapter 1 – Realizing My Difference

Missing Out

The love bead summer of 1969, howling with Woodstock free love and the feminist bra-burning movement, made barely a sound on the backyard patio of my neighbor's house. I, along with my friends, five of us total, ages ranging from 10 to 13, did not outwardly scorn the changing face of femininity. We simply put our efforts into the tried-and-true success path. Each of us quietly sought our ideal of the perfect mentor through our dedication to *her* game.

Sindy, my next-door neighbor and one of my closest friends, owned the game. From its off-white cover, edges trimmed in the soiled wear of cherished use to its game board of abundant promise, the *Barbie® Queen of the Prom™* game lay before us holding everything dear our child minds could conjure up.

Regal in her demeanor. Perfect in her figure and beauty, she was the ideal. She never faltered in living the dream. She was the epitome of grace and stature. The cachet of hope for my awkward preadolescent clumsiness.

As Sindy spread the board and laid it on the table, I could feel a warmth, anticipation, begin just below my heart, like a small ember of energy, projecting slowly throughout my body. Heart thumping energy. A smile inched upward on the edges of my mouth. My eyes shouted expectancy. The *Game* lay before us.

My eyes landed on the cards depicting the young men. Who would I get as my boyfriend? I had a favorite and it was not the popular choice amongst my friends.

"I wanna play."

"Me too."

"Oh, me, me."

"I am definitely playing," Sindy ended the round robin

of claimed spots that interrupted my dream state. Four players were the maximum.

The players took their places. Smiles on every face. My mind rolled around the consequences of my inaction. The emptiness echoing my fate. I wouldn't be able to go to school, join a club, earn money. Go to the prom. The boy I longed for would belong to someone else. And they would go steady. I knew the game well.

Missing out meant watching the contest dormant from the sidelines. The muscles twitch with anticipation, but that is their only movement. You can't expect to be good at anything unless you practice. And I was determined to practice. The stakes were too high. This was exercise for life.

Blinking hard, I said, "but I wanna play too."

"You can play next time," Sindy said,

"Next time . . . " I mumbled, feeling the despair of those two words as they left my lips.

I would watch this game, as I would watch many others. Each time with an isolation that bounced through my desire, echoing what I already feared was reality.

Loneliness

If loneliness was a stalwart of my preadolescence, it had its beginnings early in my life. One of my first memories was as a toddler. My younger brother's first birthday. A seemingly happy event, I felt the cold table beneath the outer portion of my thighs. The kitchen table hard against my calves. My legs sprawled in front of me, just short of crosswise. My younger brother, just a baby, sat next to me moving his arms up and down in rapid succession. My father grabbed my hand in his larger, stronger grip. He set our joined hands down on top of my brother's flailing wrist.

"You have to hold his arm still," he said, backing up, camera in one hand, free arm pointing toward the table where we sat. "Keep his hand away from the candle."

The attention on my brother. Me sitting by him in my dress I didn't dare get dirty – the Sunday one, the one I wear when we go see Grandma and Grandpa. Just in front, between us was a cake, barely fitting the plate on which it sat, slathered with frosting, a lone burning effuse to his special day.

I must do what I'm told. Surely love comes to the do-gooder. An early lesson in following expectations. My eyes went down to the thing I needed to protect him from. Lit, it danced to rhythm far off in the distance. It took me under its power.

"Okay, that's good . . . "

I clung to his words as praise. I had done something good. He said so. I could rest in that for now.

The click of the camera signaled the end of my responsibility. The emptiness remained.

Attraction

I would face one of the first crushing disappointments of my young life when I found out that my two closest friends from junior high were going off to attend another high school. Sindy was many things to me, next door neighbor, owner of *the Game* and center of our neighborhood group, and my best friend at school. Stacy was her friend initially, but by the end of ninth grade, the three of us had formed a special bond. We had spent all our time together. These girls were my lifeblood, my talisman of comfort in the scary world of being a teenager. Being intensely shy, I didn't look forward to meeting the challenge of a new school setting, especially high school, without any friends by my side.

My saving grace came when a girl, prior to that time I had only been acquainted with, called me early into our summer vacation. She wanted to go bike riding with me.

I was surprised by her invitation but thrilled. Maybe I

would make a new friend going into high school. Saving me from my deeply pitted well of friendlessness. An antidote to my anticipated loneliness.

When she arrived, she told me we were headed off to a nearby park where she was meeting up with her new boyfriend. A wave of disappointment fell over me. I had been the odd girl out before. Sindy and another of my neighborhood friends had paired up with real boys a year prior and neither of those guys enjoyed having me around. The razing I got from them was merciless and hurtful. I didn't relish getting into a similar situation. But I was already on the hook. And if I was going to be a new friend, I could see no way around this.

Fortunately, I did not face the same problem. This young man was very nice and didn't seem to hold the same animosity toward me for being the intruder. *Unfortunately*, I found myself facing a different problem growing out of the situation. And this one, by far, was worse.

We sat together in the park, the three of us. Them sitting against a tree talking, me on my belly, elbows planted firmly in the grass, staring at the ground. Pulling up blades of grass and chewing on the ends. I bit into those tender roots trying unsuccessfully to blend into the earth they came from.

He talked to me, tried to include me in the conversation. Trying hard to smile, I was surprised at the kind attention. It was very different from my previous experience.

My eyes landed on his hands. Arms wrapped around his bended knees, his hands gripped one another tightly, holding him steady in the folded nature of his body. If I kept looking at his hands, I could avoid looking into his eyes. The last thing I wanted to do was to fall into those eyes.

My demeanor soon lost all its guard and soared from resistive to softly open. Within moments, that openness shifted once again. My heartbeat began to shuffle throughout my chest and neck, interfering with any attempt at methodical breathing. Strange sensations ran through me, not just my mind, but my body also. Tingling quivers. Hyperventilating nerve endings. Internal fireworks just below my skin's surface. The creep of a forest fire through my flesh up the sides of my neck. These sensations seemed to explode into my awareness, all at once, in exaggerated tenor.

I wasn't sure exactly what this new strangeness meant. Its power scared me while at the same time titillated me. Inexperienced as I was with grown-up yearnings, I knew one thing – I was drawn to him. I had been attracted to boys before. But not like this. The intensity sent my mind searching for a way to slip behind the tree out of sight. Escape whatever it was that was happening to me.

Instead, I wrung my legs back and forth behind me kicking away the prickly nerve endings and quaking muscles. Unable to find an exit, I looked away with the naive hope that neither one of them would see the red percolating from my neck up to my cheeks.

I could stand it no longer. I jumped to my feet and moved to the swing-set near where they remained seated under the tree. I needed to separate myself from the physical closeness. And, if possible, the intimacy of that nearness. Pulling back hard on the chains of the swing helped unleash nervous energy that had nowhere to go. *I am her friend,* I repeated to myself, *what's happening in me isn't right.* But I couldn't push these yet unnamed feelings out of my mind. Surely, this could not last. Surely, I could overcome this crazy awkwardness, even with its strange new sensations.

Chemistry Ignited

Awareness. I had plenty. But being aware of all the sensual changes in my body held few clues to their meaning. It didn't tell me what exactly was going on inside of me.

The world was a puberty-induced firework display. All happening within the walls of my skin. The sensations, twinges, little pleasure geysers, would appear seemingly out of nowhere. They were not unpleasant, but baffling, and in their strangeness, I shrank from their power while craving their presence. In an awkward sense of balance, I savored the delicious intensity of new feeling while at the same time felt miserable. A strange and confusing state.

Still, I couldn't wait for school to start. My initial apprehension had faded into pins-and-needles anticipation.

Greens and Blues

But summer wasn't over yet. One afternoon, I sat on the front porch with one of my favorite pastimes. Dandelions sparsely populated the yard, making a distinct contrast high above the mown evenness of the grass. The columbines from my mother's flower garden just below the kitchen window swayed their maroon and purple heads gently in response to the breeze. Slight as it was, it was welcome on this afternoon.

A small patch of ill-advised green grew out of that garden in our front yard that summer. The vine wound its way out of the garden's edge and clung close to the inverted corner of the bottom step leading to the front door. Inching past the brick base of the porch. Sticking closely to the masonry as if to protect itself, each day it inched further along some unspoken path. Alone. Defying convention. Until one day it stopped, burst into flower, then began to germinate a nub. The nub grew defiantly larger and larger each day.

The watermelon vine's aberration, the result of a family member's after dinner snack, was an accident we chose not to abort. We all simply stepped over it. Choosing to ignore it. Until the nub reached maturation. When its sweetness called to us, we devoured it.

Back on the porch, a few steps above the vine, I sat. Stringing small beads onto necklace string, I absorbed the color around me allowing it to penetrate first my head, then down into my heart, and out through my hands. The colors of summer guiding my fingers as they worked.

Spurts of red, orange, purple flowering in every yard. Sky overhead with no weather to obstruct it save an occasional billow of cloud. Blue. White. Earth rising from the ground to meet it. Brown. The grays of concrete in an urban area. All set on a background of lawn, shrub, and tree. The greens of summer. Adamant green. Bead by bead, the impact of the last days of my summer vacation catapulted its way into the design of my necklace.

There was very little traffic on our normally busy street that afternoon. No vehicle had ventured past as I strung bead-after-bead into place. The quiet adding its own color to my creation. Into the peace, I worked until I glimpsed something that caught my attention. On the edge of my sight. Movement. A bicyclist peddling by.

Slowly I looked up. There was something familiar in the figure on the bike. My summer friend's boyfriend. Or was it my imagination? I looked a little too long. The bicyclist didn't return my gaze. Instead, he rose and pushed more violently on the pedals.

Tickles like the brush of spider feet scampered all around my stomach, pushing out the spell of color. My fingers refused to move. Eyes darting up and down to their own nervous rhythm, sending information in spurts to my brain. The moment more like a thousand moments packed tightly into compression.

When the bicyclist was out of sight, I scolded myself. Not only was I thinking about this guy when I didn't want to, but I was seeing him when he wasn't there. Through careful, compact analysis I had decided it could not be him. Or maybe I just didn't want it to be him. To this day, I don't know.

I looked back down at my necklace laying limp and loose on its string. I desperately wanted to go back to the previous minute and relive it differently. Regain my whimsy.

But my will wouldn't cooperate. I picked up a blue bead and stared at it. A forced distraction to the enormity of my apprehension. Its blueness drew me in. The deep summer sky blue was gone. In its place rainy day blue, a dampness of spirit. I threw the necklace into the bead box, carelessly closed the lid, and went inside the house. Leaving summer's color to its own expression.

Sensitivity

"You're too sensitive."

The chasm that was communication between my mother and I had deep walls. Not often would I venture into its hollowness. I preferred instead to retreat to the comfort of my room. In its silence I could slough off the immensity of concern. Corner the nuances of feeling that assaulted me. Whittle down the conglomerate mass into easier-to-digest pieces.

Still, there were times when I needed an older, wiser opinion to help me see what my young eyes naively missed. This growing feeling toward a boy I hardly knew was one of those times. But there were moments in the past when I would go to her. The "you're too sensitive" line seemed to be her answer on every occasion.

Being "too sensitive" was the all too undesirable trait in my eyes. The trait to be pushed aside, hidden, and extinguished if possible. If not possible, then to be camouflaged. The devil trait. Staining my interaction with everyone I encountered.

The threat of this pronouncement triggered my silence. I vowed to keep my feelings secret. Bury them deep within me. Find the solution on my own.

I Don't Fit In

It wasn't just the sensitivity thing. I didn't feel like I fit in anywhere in my family. My father was the center of it, although you might not suspect that from the complaints he made. "No one listens to me." "My opinion doesn't matter." By the time I got to junior high, he rarely worked. Often sitting home with head in hand, sick look on his face, demanding everyone's attention with so little as a whimper. His "sinus headaches," diagnosed by a depression-era doctor, caused so much distress that he would often groan in pain.

My mother orbited around him and his every wish. We would often take trips to nowhere. Dad needed to get out of the house, she would say, so we would load ourselves into the car and drive. Sometimes we would go to a park, the mountains, or a lake. Often, we had no real destination but would end up at a small coffee shop where my father would order a strong cup and soon feel better.

My brother seemed to shrug this behavior off, having no seeming concern. My attempts to talk to him about behavior that seemed different from other families I knew dismissed as he regained his freedom and ran off to play. Leaving me the stranger I was to my own family.

At least when I found myself at school, life felt a little more normal.

Conflicting Emotion

I started my first day of high school to Helen Reddy's *I am Woman. Strong, invincible*, I echoed to myself, with the hope that it would take.

To my surprise, I quickly coalesced with new friends. As did my summer friend. She and her boyfriend had broken up within weeks of our first encounter at the park. We had continued our forays to the park, my game of Monopoly bouncing off the top of my handlebars. We'd spent hours playing the game, watchful of our surroundings, should there be something or someone of interest nearby. Now, in the crowd of new possibilities, we weren't spending every minute together.

Though we focused on different friends, different interests, my summer friend would occasionally seek me out to talk about her former boyfriend. Flashing between anger and tearful sadness, she mourned with a force deeper than what my own desires might expose. Compassion for her loss wrestled with my joy at his single status. I scolded that joy with a steaming hot blast of guilt. My dichotomy of mind shuffled back and forth with the speed of a pinwheel on a blustery day.

I had been working hard at pushing the thoughts of him, of that first day in the park out of my mind. And the guilt of the secret I kept from her. But I also knew she needed someone to talk to. I didn't know why she chose me. Probably because I was there with her during the summer romance. I listened to her talk. The tears pooling in her eyes. The sting pricking my own. Her tears would mutate over into anger. That anger infiltrating my muscles. Making them tense. Sending anger messages into my brain. My anger grew toward him too as I watched her heart break anew, day after day. The rift of broken heart spreading its inviolable torment beyond its borders of origin. My permeable borders giving way to its infiltrating my own vulnerability.

Reserved Regret

Half time. Sitting on the bleacher bench taking in the whole venue, I knew on this night, at least, I was happy. I loved going to my high school football games. Harmonious to my longed-for lifestyle. The gameboard of Sindy's back porch in real life. The thrill of being part of the reality rather than vicariously living through it using object cards.

On this night there was a gentle mistiness that hung over the area. A hazy veil of white tinged my view in every direction. I wondered if this was what it felt like to be in the center of a cloud.

Being there was a requirement for me. I was in the band. Wearing an ill-fitting wool uniform and leather captain's hat. Despite my attire, my nerves tingled like little twinkling Christmas lights. After the halftime performance, my follow bandmates scattered in different directions. Feeling a sudden thirst, I left my flute laying crosswise on the bench and headed toward the concession stand for a cold drink.

Upon my return, I placed my cup on the vacant seat in front of me so I could adjust my flute back into place. As I sat folding the instrument into its position on my lap, I glimpsed an arm in my peripheral vision. The hand moving slowly, methodically toward my drink, cupped into a grasping position. I followed its origin slowly to the face I least expected. I froze.

Where had he come from? Although I tended to be forever aware of his presence, he'd snuck by my observance this night. I hadn't even been thinking about him.

The arm stopped moving. His eyes moved to meet mine. I lifted an eyebrow. His lips moved ever so slightly into the start of a smile. My forehead pinned together in questioning lines, I could form no cohesive response.

"You can have it," I said, nodding my head toward the cup, "if you want it."

The arm stopped its march within inches of the cup. He mumbled something that sounded like a refusal to my offer and turned his back to me.

Okay, that was stupid, I thought. But what could've, would've, should've I have said? I stared at the back of his head, wishing he would turn around. But hoping he would not. I was caught between wanting that boyfriend card and something that said *No, do you really want to do that*? With thoughts of my summer friend's still enduring pain bouncing off my conscience. Her agonized heart running through my core.

This crush was starting to turn on me.

<u>Trying to be Heard</u>

Growing into adolescence had up to this point been a challenge. It was about to get a bit more complicated. At 16, my menstrual period was still lost. Something was terribly wrong. I could sense it deep within an undefined suspicion. Though I rarely confided in my mother, I now forced myself to approach her on this subject. She reluctantly made an appointment with her gynecologist for me.

Mom and I both sat in the doctor's examining room waiting impatiently for him to come in. My mother, looking agitated said, "I know what he's going to say. You're just a late-bloomer."

I looked toward my feet. "There's something wrong," I mumbled, "I just know it."

My mother sighed heavily and looked at the door. We sat the rest of the time in silence.

When he arrived, he asked me to sit on his examining table and asked my mother to leave the room.

"So, you are not having your period? Is that right?" the doctor asked after she left.

"Yes," I answered, and launched into my story. By now, I had had two half-hearted periods in two years followed by nothing. Surely, this doctor whom my mother trusted and who was smiling down at me as he spoke would get to the bottom of this.

"Do you have any boyfriends?" he continued.

"Huh, what? No," I said, a little lost. My cheeks burning with insinuation. Talk as intimate as this was new to my vocabulary.

"Then, you're not having sex?"

I tried to stop my heart beating outside the confines of my chest. Return it to a normal state. "No, absolutely not." I could feel my face burning all over.

He relaxed in his chair and leaned back. "You're still

very young. It takes some girls longer than others to get regular. Give it some time."

With that he closed his file, summoned my mother back to the room, assured her that I was not pregnant, and we left not saying a word to each other. I wanted to cry. He didn't deem it necessary to do an examination. My fears were still present, and on top of that, I couldn't get an adult to take me seriously.

Dishonor

"We met the nicest girl . . ." I had drifted off into my own thoughts while my friends talked.

I loved my high school friends. Most were part of a previously established group from a nearby small town. I'd met the first of these close friends at a combined junior high concert. She sat next to me through several practices and a concert. We'd started our acquaintance talking about the clash between school colors. Her orange jacket to my red one. On my first day of high school, I'd run into her and she had introduced me to her friends They quickly accepted me into their group.

This group was now sitting together at lunchtime when another girl close to two of my friends joined us. These three were competing in a Junior Miss pageant. Telling the rest of our group about the practices they were attending leading up to the night of their competition.

I listened as they gushed about a new acquaintance they'd met. She was from our rival high school, was a cheerleader, and had struck them as the greatest thing since the introduction of great things into the world.

"She's the sweetest person you could ever want to meet," praised one of my pageant-participating friends. When they mentioned her name, I perked to the surprise.

"Stacy," I said, "She's been a friend of mine since

junior high." I warmed to hearing Stacy's name again. She *was* one of the nicest people I had ever met, and I'd thought of her often.

My entire table of friends turned in unison to look at me. "Sindy and Stacy and I spent all our time together in ninth grade," I said in an unusual display of outgoing fervor. I glanced about the circle watching the smiles grow bigger still. Of course, they would all like Stacy. Only the rarest of human beings would find fault in her. "You have to say 'hi' for me," I said.

I'd grieved my two junior high friends. The faint stain of friendships past lingering in a melancholy undercurrent of loss throughout my high school years. My current friends' answer to my request was unanimous. Smiling, the three agreed they would be sure to tell her.

After lunch, as I drifted to my next class, I indulged in memories. Chain-linked by common experience the bond is stronger than three alone. This was the nature of connection to me. And to me, this was a special bond. I had longed to go into high school with both, but they were attending the other high school, my school's cross-town rival. These last two and half years, they had been together, still in each other's lives. I separate from them. *Wow, Stacy, a cheerleader*, I thought, *good for her.*

That warmth of remembrance would last no longer than a week. It stalled one morning as I was coming from band, when I saw my two friends outside the choir room talking to their pageant friend. I stopped to join them. They were discussing the pageant practice they had gone to the night before. "Did you tell her 'hi' for me?" I interjected when the conversation turned to Stacy once again.

Silence. Frowns replaced the previously joy-filled faces of my friends. No one was speaking. I might as well have been outside during a blizzard. "Well?" I said as I tried to quell the suddenly awakened nerves in my body. A sense of something gone wrong. A feeling of dread.

The three looked at each other with the gravity of a funeral. When they finally spoke, it was nearly in unison. "She doesn't know you."

An involuntary swallow hit my throat as I took in those words. *No, No* echoed in my mind. I looked into the eyes of the girls who delivered these words. I studied those eyes, trying to disseminate what they had to say. Pity, embarrassment for me, uneasiness of the situation. My cheeks flushed. My knees pitched slightly before I caught them back in place.

"No," I said, "That's not true. Sindy and Stacy and I were like the three musketeers in junior high." I hoped that last part didn't sound like a question. It felt like one as I heard it rolling out of my mouth. A surge of energy, the first blush of anger mixed with already mature bewilderment, rose in me. A rush of unaccustomed assertiveness took over. "Tell her again," I commanded. *She couldn't have forgotten me, could she?* "Please, ask her again," I said, softer this time.

The three looked at each other. Hesitantly this time. The previous condoling looks had not faded from their faces. Shame burned down through the layers of my skin, deep into my heart. I looked up as they all agreed that they would tell her the next time they saw her. I mumbled something about getting to my next class on time and left them.

Could she really have forgotten me? No, I assured myself, once she thought about it, she would remember. It wasn't *that* long ago. I remembered her. The memory of both my friends still as fresh in the narrow interim as if it had never occurred. The next few days I spent in melancholy as the spurn of rejection lingered in my mind.

Finally, I was able to approach my friends when I knew they had been through another practice. As I suspected, the remnants of pageant practice were the discussion. As I sat down next to them, they quickly changed the subject. I wasn't going to let it pass. "So, did you see Stacy at your practice?" I pushed the words from my gut out of my mouth. I wasn't sure I wanted to know, but deep down I did. Hesitantly the two looked at each other. This time they did not look at me. "Yes," one of them said, "She doesn't know you."

I weighed the response. The three girls I had entrusted with my message were honest, trustworthy people. If they said it, it happened. All I could conclude was that Stacy had forgotten me. How unmemorable was I? How can you spend an entire school year of your life hanging around with someone, and completely forget their existence? Apparently, it was possible.

Disappointment and anger pooled in my mood. I waffled between being angry with her for the offense and being angrier at myself for believing in our friendship. For believing in myself that I was not forgettable as a friend. When, in fact, I was. In response, I tried to avoid people the rest of the day. Letting the pain sift slowly into my consciousness. Feeling the crush of disappointment wrap me round, and slowly squeeze me into breathlessness.

As the days rolled into weeks, the dampness I felt turned to acrimony at the thought of her. The acrimony turned to grief. I began to hope I would never again run into her. But forgetting her was not easy. Neither was forgiving myself.

Finishing High School

My senior year was coming to an end, and I felt a sense of remorse. I'd gone through high school without a date, attended no prom, lived a nonexistent romantic life. I couldn't even look forward to going to college. My mother had spent the better part of my high school years discouraging further education. When I started applying to college, she stopped discouraging and came right out with it. "We can't afford to send you to college." End of story.

That was in my junior year, so I turned to the school's

vocational segment. I signed up for Office Education in my senior year. To become a secretary. I needed a skill to go into the job market when I graduated at the end of the year. As part of that program, the school placed me in a part-time job working at another school to get work experience. The last couple of months of high school academia I spent working in the nurse's office of one of the two junior highs in town.

One day, during my last week of work at the school, I was walking down the hall on my way out after my shift was over. At the end of the long hall, I glimpsed another girl around my own age. I couldn't make out a face, but she wore the distinctive color and uniform of our rival high school's cheerleader squad. And she was walking my direction. That sight sent ripples through my inner reaches.

Please don't let it be Stacy. Please don't let it be Stacy. The mantra tornadoed through my thoughts. As the figure got closer and I could make out her face, *Please don't let it be Stacy* still echoed in my head as I realized it was her. There was no escape. No hallway to turn into, no open classroom in which to hide.

What should I do? bumped into the *Please don't let it be Stacy thoughts*. I was trapped.

She doesn't remember me! The flash of dishonor hit just before she reached me. The answer became simple. I could just walk on by her without so much as a look in her direction. She didn't remember me so it would just be like passing a stranger in the hall. The moment would be over quickly, like ripping off a band aid. I relaxed as we passed shoulder-to-shoulder.

Up to that time there was no discernible look of recognition on her face, no gasp of realization in her eyes. But as moment we approached each other and passed shoulder-to-shoulder, I saw from my peripheral vision a slight, barely noticeable glance my way. At the end of which she stopped walking and turned my way. Her face held a look of curiosity, unfamiliar curiosity.

I walked on, anxious to get past the band aid pull sting. As I walked down the hall, her face lay frozen in my mind's eye. From the distance of moments passed, I studied her face. Her eyes appeared to search. A frown created lines circling her eyes, her lips were parted quizzically. I could almost hear her say, "Do I know you?"

Through the rancor I had felt over the last couple of months, I tried to ignore the unsettling discomfort of the face I'd walked past, the one emblazoned in my mind. I pushed it aside, unwilling to revisit the pain of my initial rejection.

Movie of the Week

"Can I do it after the movie is over?" I asked my mother. She had just asked me to run something she had borrowed back over to the next-door neighbors. It was just a few minutes before a movie that I had been looking forward to for several days was about to come onto the television. "Dad will turn the TV off if I am not here when the movie starts."

"No," she said without looking at me. "I want you to do it now. It won't take but a minute."

"Please," I begged. "Let me do it later."

"No," came her answer, "Do it now. Dad won't turn the TV off, I promise."

I dawdled no more. If I could run fast, maybe I could get back before he discovered the tv sitting idle with no one watching it. I knew my father's opinion on the subject. I'd heard it plenty of times. *If you're not watching the tv, it goes off.* Those words coming through my mind in my father's voice. Behind the proclamation was his opinion that nothing but sports were worth watching on tv. Movies didn't qualify as acceptable watching.

I grabbed the item from the table where my mother had placed it. Out the door I flew. I loved our next-door neighbors.

They were a friendly older couple whose daughters lived in other states. They would want to talk for a while. She answered the door and asked me in.

"I need to get back," I smiled, hoping I was not being rude.

As I ran back to our front door, I hoped I had not missed much of the start of the movie. I loved movies but I was not often given permission to go to the movie theater. Then one of the television channels started featuring a movie of the week. This week's feature was one I was anticipating for days.

I opened the door and looked quickly to my left where the television lay silent. Off. My vision moved front and center where my father stood glaring at me. He said nothing. He didn't have to. His eyes spoke in daggers. After an elongated pause, he turned and left.

I looked to my right where my mother was still working in the kitchen. When my father was completely out of sight, I turned toward my mother, "I knew he would turn it off," I said more resigned than angry.

She refused to meet my eyes with her own. "Turn it back on," her terse words, like blocks slowly building a stone wall, jabbed at me "if you have to."

I stood in position, not moving. I wanted with everything in me to watch that movie. But if I turned the tv back on at that moment, I would make both even angrier than they already were. The decision was easy. I walked past the tv, into my room, closing the door behind me.

The Headache Companion

I was hyper-aware of the things that my father did that I didn't like. Things that I swore I would never do or become. Fight as I might, there was one circumstance I felt I had no control of. There was nothing I could do about.

The summer I had met my high school crush I had

begun to get dull headaches. They would start in the afternoon, worsen as I spent time in the sun, and only be relieved by the night's sleep. They were intermittent at first, but by the end of the summer, I could fully expect to see them appear every afternoon.

I had begun to raid my father's supply of aspirin to stop them. Helpful at first, they soon became resistant to the medicine. Throughout high school, they had grown in strength, becoming a daily presence from morning to night. At times, they would explode into pain so deep, I would retreat to my bedroom for a nap.

I tried ignoring them, but it's no easy task to dismiss pain. Physical or otherwise.

Chapter 2 - Setting the Journey in Motion

Beginnings

I sat in my chair in the hospital's Medical Record Department. This was the place at which I chose to catapult into my adult life. From my position in the nurse's office at the junior high, I easily got a job as Inpatient Clerk. If you believe in synchronistic events, as I do, I was destined to get this job. Not only did I simply walk into to it easily, but it would start a string of coincidental events. Meaningful coincidences Carl Jung would call them.

And apparently the forces in life that plan these things were impatient to begin. I replaced a woman who was nine months pregnant. The department was desperate to get someone at the desk, so much so that they practically pleaded with me to start immediately. My first day at work was the day after my high school graduation.

My desk was no more than six feet away from Cecilia, a synchronistic event in and of herself. Cecilia was the Assistant Director and a Medical Records Technician doing much of the coding for the department. My desk so close, I sat within earshot. Unknown to her, Cecilia would become my chosen mentor. Single like myself, she had a breezy charm that seemed to pull men to her. Confidence and a self-assured personality were built into her character. She was deep within and a vital part of the hospital's group of single people. I surmised from the beginning; this was someone I could learn from.

In the few days since I'd known her, I had begun to revere her. In an unhealthy, careless, distracted way. On this day, though, I would see the first cracks to fracture my admiration of her.

I could hear Cecilia and the employee next to her

discuss many of the records she coded. That day, one case was particularly incendiary to her. It caught my attention. This patient was a woman who often visited the Emergency Room and subsequently had been admitted to the hospital on numerous occasions. She presented with excruciating head pain and was often given powerful drugs to help her resolve her agony. When that failed, she would return to the ER again and again until she was admitted as an inpatient. Most of those times required stays longer than a week. She had recently been discharged from one of these prolonged stays.

Cecilia spoke in an irritated manner, flopping open the chart, straining it apart at its two-pronged heading, and writing fast and hard on its interior. She and our co-worker were discussing this patient's confidential medical notes that lay in front of her.

". . . just wants attention . . . an excuse to get drugs . . . better use for the room . . . pathetic. . ."

I cringed at the words being used to describe her and her situation. It was clear that Cecilia and I had two very different viewpoints. As I heard the details of the patient's stay, strong feelings gripped me. A sense of agony, desperation, physical pain. The sense was so powerful, it made my eyes sting to wetness. Cecilia clung to her assertion that the woman had no authentic reason to seek medical help.

I paused what I was doing and looked in their direction. "So, you don't think her pain is real?" I could feel the queasiness begin to fill my stomach as I spoke. I knew from personal experience that headache pain was real. Unwelcome. Jarring life from proactive to reactive in a matter of moments.

"She claims to have a migraine, but all she really wants is drugs," was Cecilia's emphatic response. "She's a drug addict."

There it was – the *m* word, migraine, associated with drug addiction. And at the same time a full summation of most of healthcare's opinion, at that time, of people who came to them for help with it.

I was deeply aware of this reaction and belief. Since my childhood brush with headaches, they had only progressed. On a subconscious level, this terrified me. I, too, was fearful that my only recourse would be strong drugs. I had resolved to myself that I would find another solution, even as the headaches seemed to only get worse. I also feared that one day these milder daily headaches would turn so much fiercer. Migraine was a cruel enemy I hoped to avoid.

Fear stopped the conversation. I didn't want to see where it would go from there. I shored up my resolve to keep my problem quiet until I could find a resolution on my own for it. In our town, the medical community was small enough to warrant keeping secrets or risk becoming another target as was the woman Cecilia found so unforgivable.

Acupuncture

My nerves tingled. My heart thumped in my chest making reverberating jolts in odd places on the rest of my body. Acupuncture is a well-known and widely accepted form of alternative medicine today. In 1976, most people considered it a form of eastern witchcraft.

Still here I sat having driven 60 miles one direction to the only acupuncturist in our state. I don't know if the fear of my headache secret seeping into the medical community, or becoming Cecilia's next target for ridicule, was the greater catalyst for me taking baby steps into this unknown art. But something other than my car drove me here to this man's house. A dogged, invisible energy attached to my will.

Being the life novice that I was, I hadn't asked for any sort of credentials. I wouldn't even have known where to begin. The medical school that would teach how to stick needles into assorted unrelated places in a person's body to gain relief from pain was a concept beyond my grasp.

"Have you done this long?" I asked.

"Long enough," he said. "I've helped a lot of people."

We discussed the headaches I was experiencing. To my relief, he did not urge me to seek a medical opinion first. He explained that he would be placing needles into acupuncture points that correlated to certain meridians that ran through my body. The description for the cure still eluding my understanding. If it worked, I didn't care how.

I reclined on a chair that curved in a gentle S from my head to my toes. I clasped my hands together and rested them on my belly while he stuck 2-inch-long needles mostly into my ears. I lay in this position for some time, wondering when it was going to start working.

I would spend several weeks making my sojourn. After what seemed like thousands of pokes, I had to resign myself to the fact that this form of treatment held no hope for me. I had to look elsewhere.

Paper Doll Chase

Creativity comes from within. It pushes you to grow. It exposes your vulnerability. For some, it is a drive born of passion that grabs you and won't let go. Without creativity, we wouldn't be where we are today, prospering from the inventions of creative people whose drive wouldn't let them rest. As a youngster, I didn't know this nor did I care. All I knew was that there was a force within me whose energy I had to give in to.

Around the age of 8, I received a folder of paper dolls. The dolls were troll likenesses. Short, squat little human-like figures with large, exaggerated eyes, ears, nose, and bellybuttons, colorful hair shooting straight into the air and a smile like a circle cut in half. I was thrilled.

I carefully punched out the little dolls and cut out their clothes. One round of trying on their store-bought clothing, paper apparel included with my set, held my childish interest for no more time than it took to try the outfits on once. But I couldn't put the dolls away. I wanted more clothes than were included in my 29¢ folder.

My child's mind contemplated the severe lack of clothing. Even if I could convince someone to buy me more clothes, I knew there were probably no more paper clothing made for these little dolls. There was only one answer to my problem – I had to make the clothes myself.

I jumped to my feet and ran off to gather the things I needed to start making more clothing. Paper, crayons, scissors. I set to work laying out design after design. I barely got one outfit made before inspiration for the next outfit popped into my head.

The joy of playing with the dolls became lost in my activity. Replacing it was the joy of creating their wardrobe. Idea after idea popped into my head. I could not keep up with the ideas. The dolls no longer ranked as my highest concern. They were simply the models. Day wear. Evening wear. Casual wear. Swimwear. Even costumes.

When I was designing, the world transformed. Time ceased to exist. Nothing else existed except my receiving my inspiration and applying it to the finished product. Bringing about each new idea. Allowing my child's fabrications to flow into fruition.

I may have been consciously driven by the desire to the perfect relationship and the perfect family, but I was subconsciously drawn to building the images drawn from my mind's own doodles. A rhythm in me, effortless moment-to-moment. Lost in the thrill of giving life to ideas.

In my post high school doldrum of clerical work, I longed to indulge this childhood passion. Transform it from designing paper doll clothing into designing real people clothing. I began to investigate how I could do this.

Fashion Design School

I never did anything on a whim. I always contemplated every decision until I was sure of my response. Going to fashion design school was as close as I'd ever gotten to being spontaneous. I chose a school from the back pages' ad of a magazine, a private school. Applied. Got accepted. Told everyone I was going off to school to become a fashion designer.

Now, here I was. Possessions packed into two trunks on the day of my departure.

Sitting in the bus terminal, my nerves were a jangled mess. I was surprised that my parents wanted to take me to the bus station. Since I'd defied their edict and chose to go to college even though they were against it. They hadn't put up too much of a resistance when I told them I needed transportation there.

Now, I wondered if I should have tried harder to find an alternate method. My father sat hunched in one of the bus-terminal chairs, slightly slouched, his finger alongside his face, chin leaning on his hand, elbow propped on the arm of the chair. Staring into space. My father's demeanor made my nerves shoot to their ends and reverberate just below the surface of my skin.

My mother, whose attention was always on pleasing my father, was jumpy. She stood, then sat next to him, then jumped up to fetch a coffee, or snack from the vending machine, or to seek advice from the clerk behind the counter. Always returning to him with her offerings.

Just get on the bus. That's all I want to do, just get on the bus. I chanted this anthem to myself with no resolution to the uneasiness going on within me.

I had so many reasons for wanting to do this. Learn more about designing. Have at least one year of college experience. But mostly, I wanted to get away. Get away from my parents' home and its curious dynamics.

I tried to avoid thinking about my responsibility to my parents to stick around. They didn't want me to go to college. I'd known that for years. I opposed their wishes. And that act had resulted in so much dread that I questioned whether it was what I should've done.

Just get on the bus. The length of each succeeding minute grew exponentially. I tried not to look at them. *Just get . . .on the bus. Get on the bus.*

Progression

My stay at the fashion design school was short. One year. Disillusionment took over when the school did not turn out to be what I hoped it would be. With a gnawing ache in my stomach, I returned to the hospital and asked for my job back.

At the beginning of my employment at the hospital, I progressed from my first clerk position into a pool of typists transcribing doctors' recordings of medical records. The hospital welcomed me back into the transcription room, and I resumed my life where I left a year earlier.

Everything was the same, except that the headaches I had were getting worse. They were and had been a constant companion for a couple of years now. Growing more intense and more frequent. I tried to treat the pain by taking more aspirin.

My concern for this increased aspirin reliance grew along with my increasing headache presence. I knew I was losing the battle and didn't have a clue about how to even begin to change it. If things did not resolve on their own, I would have to see a doctor.

The headaches were not my only health concern. I was nineteen now, and I still had not seen a normal period beyond the half-days each when I was 14 and 16.

I didn't want to return to my mother's gynecologist, and

felt a little apprehensive contemplating using any of the doctors with whom I worked, sharing this intimate secret. If I dared to share this problem, how would I be perceived? Could I continue working at the hospital? Dangling in the back of my head, too, was my own persistent scornful taunt. A deficiency in what makes a woman a woman.

A friend suggested her gynecologist to me. He practiced in a neighboring town, and only occasionally admitted patients to our hospital. I promptly made an appointment.

<u>The Shattered Swan</u>

We shuffled into the cafeteria. Everyone from Medical Records, Accounting, HR – all the ancillary departments that support the medical staff. It was a required meeting. Four or five of us to a table, our department took up three or four tables. As we settled in, a fellow employee walked from table to table handing each of us a sample product.

Lorelei, another transcriptionist, sat to my left, and Cecilia sat two to my right or practically across from me.

"What's this?" someone from another table asked. "A gift to keep," the bearer of gifts smiled. Our gifts consisted of sample-sized personal care products.

As the meeting started, I focused on the speaker. Within minutes and without warning my focus lapsed. In its place was a disparate flash of discomfort. A knowing within the confines of my perception. Something on the table had changed. I reacted to the knowing by looking down. I was right. My gift was now in front of Lorelei, and her gift, a bottle of mouth wash, lay in front of me. Though they were only a couple inches apart from each other, they had without-a-doubt exchanged positions.

Lorelei was, from the moment I met her, one of those people that sent fingernails down the chalkboard of my interaction with her. She could look me in the eye and smile, and while anyone looking on might find it a warm and inviting exchange, I would feel unease explode in my abdomen. Her eyes lacked the warmth of kind expression. The softness of sincerity. Instead, they would pierce me deeper than any knife could cut. Invisible in their wounding, but deadly in their result.

Beatrice was our supervisor, and Lorelei's hatred of Beatrice was well known to the transcription room. Lorelei's loathing attitude toward Beatrice baffled me. Beatrice was a kind person and hands-off manager. I could find no personal nor professional reason to dislike her. In fact, I liked her immensely.

On Beatrice's desk was a small glass swan. A cherished memento from a Hawaiian vacation. She kept her paper clips in the hollowed out back of this swan. Whenever Beatrice left the room, Lorelei would start her usual discourse on how much she hated *that* ugly swan. She swore up and down that one day she would break it into a million pieces. She went into her rant with a grin and ecstatic laughter. The other women in our transcription room laughed at her comedic diatribe. I'd flash a forced smile and turn back with keen interest to my work. I was sure Lorelei was taking out her feelings for Beatrice on that poor swan.

Lorelei and Cecilia were close friends.

Immediately after seeing the switch during our staff meeting, I glanced up to see the ends of Cecilia's lips curve slightly upwards and her eyes fix on Lorelei. Reactively, my eyes darted toward Lorelei. She was stone-faced, staring intently at the speaker.

I returned the gifts to their original places, giving Lorelei back her mouth wash, and turned my attention back to the speaker. It was only a few minutes before I sensed the same dread of something has changed. I looked down in front of me where the bottle of mouth wash lay on its back in front of me.

Though it was sample-sized I could read the words blaring at me: *Kills the germs that cause bad breath.*

I couldn't look at either Cecilia or Lorelei. I pulled the bottle of mouth wash to my lap and stared at it. As my cheeks burned, I ran my fingers along the curved side of the bottle, feeling its hardness, willing it to go away. Willing myself to go away. I swallowed hard to stop the emotion irritating my eyes. When its sting subsided, I stared at the speaker. Eyes in place, ears useless.

After the meeting, I run-walked to the Ladies Room and an empty stall. I drew my open palm to within an inch of my mouth and breathed hard. Then sniffed. Nothing unusual that I could tell.

I repeated this process several times, always coming up empty for smell. I didn't understand. I brushed my teeth twice a day, and always visited my dentist. I tried to chalk it up to a cruel joke, but the thought of my foul, but to me unrecognizably offensive breath, stuck in the recesses of my mind.

Further analysis would have to wait. I returned to our office to find Beatrice, wet-eyed holding the head of her swan in her hand. Lorelei, squatting on the floor, picking up tiny shards of shattered swan body and paper clips, was apologizing profusely for bumping the desk and knocking it off.

<u>Upsetting the Game Board</u>

It was with that same odd sense of sitting on the fringe of life I experienced playing the Game that accompanied me into my gynecologist's office on the day I got the news. I shifted from side to side and pretended to read the rumpled magazine I'd picked up off the table. Nervously biting my lip, I wanted the time to simultaneously hurry up and to slow down. My aspirin-abused stomach was shouting even more than usual at me.

This was my second visit. On the first, I had explained my lack of menstruation conundrum to the doctor, and he had looked pensive.

"By now you should've had a period." He spoke in low tones with serious inflection. "I am going to do a series of tests that should show us what we are dealing with."

He then had his staff draw blood and scrape the inside of my mouth with a wooden tongue depressor.

This was several months before, and most of the tests were back within days. But he had waited for results from a definitive test that had to be sent out of state for processing before contacting me again. It took this long for the results to come back.

When his staff member called me to schedule this appointment, I could not stand the suspense any longer. "What did they find?"

She paused a slow, echoless moment, then said, "You'll have to ask the doctor. I can't give you any information."

"But," I wanted to say, "this is my life. I need to know. Now." I bit back the words and made the appointment for as soon as I could instead.

Now I was sitting in his office, with cold fingers, thumbing clumsily through the light fare of a woman's magazine.

When I was finally called, I followed his nurse not back to an examination room, but to an office. His office. I wondered how many women saw the inside of this office. It seemed to be an elitist group I really wanted no part of.

He had an open folder in front of him, with paper slips of varying sizes and colors scattered about. He seemed to be studying a select number of them carefully laid out on top of the folder.

He glanced up momentarily, stone still in his features. "Sit down, Monica."

I sat. Studying static eyes gave me no clue as to what he

would say next. So, I looked around without moving my head.

Finally, he let out his breath a little too heavily, and looked up at me. His eyes were strained, and his face was stone white. "Monica, I didn't want to tell you this until I was sure."

His use of my first name to preface every sentence did nothing to ease my anguish. I squeezed the frigid arms of the chair I was sitting on in hopes that I could stop my hands from shaking.

"You have what is called premature ovarian failure syndrome . . ."

"What is that?" I could barely speak. The shaking in my hands moved to my lips.

He began discussing the workings of the female body, what was normal, what is supposed to happen, how what I have just been diagnosed with gets more common as a woman grows older but is rarely seen in a woman of my age. That, perhaps, the odds of being diagnosed so young were a million to one. How no one knows how it comes about, possibly injury as a young child, possibly just by happenstance, no one knows. He talked quickly and surely, as if spewing out facts took the focus off delivering this kind of news to a young woman.

My mind barely registered the words coming from his mouth.

The practical part of me tried hard to keep up with the facts of my present condition. The unseen part of me was a kaleidoscopic jumble of negative emotions. I had heard enough to know that death was not an expected outcome, but I had also glimpsed the tip of something I considered a worse result.

"What does that mean to me?" I said looking squarely at him, determined to give the panic I felt a name.

He sat up in his chair and fleetingly stared at me. It was a stare that went straight from his eyes to infinitely beyond me. It was a stare of failure. I sensed a doctor's resignation to the limitations of science. He turned his eyes away from me and spoke gently. "The two most important things you need to know about this is, one, you will need to be on hormone replacement therapy for a long, long time, and two," he paused, "you will never be able to get pregnant."

I left his office as if I were a silent ghost moving through a war zone. Observing without participation. I was aware of the thumping, thumping of my pulse. Clouding my breath. The only sound to reach my ears. I sat in my car calculating the cost. No children equals no family, equals no life.

Three Balloons

I likened my rise into the life I longed for to the romance of a hot air balloon adventure. To send my Game vision into flight, I relied on not one but three balloons of hope. Husband, family and good health. Although I'd watched the balloon of health start to sag with my growing headache problem, it was the violent pop of the family balloon that knocked me off my feet and sent my emotions plunging into free fall. At 19 I had just learned I was infertile. The sudden shock that was my childless realization gnawed at my already flawed self-image. I tried to push the dread that no man would want a barren woman as a wife out of my head. The remaining husband balloon could not be lost too. I could still be happy, I tried to tell myself. I believed in hope. I could still fly with one balloon intact.

I became determined to re-inflate that husband balloon. My first goal was to get more involved in the single life at the hospital. There was a thriving group of single people and Cecilia was part of it. But she had a certain standoffish demeanor, especially in her treatment of me. I looked up to her for her easy manner and popularity. She held her acceptance of me just out of my reach. Her regard was tarnished with an undertone of frost. I hoped I could banish that chilliness and turn the tide of her aloof nature enough that we might become friends.

That hope got a boost one Friday when she asked me if I wanted to come watch the hospital's team, her team, play volleyball the next day at our town's rec center. I could say I was surprised. But that wouldn't do my response justice. I was shocked by her sudden interest in my social life while at the same time feeling an inconsistency akin to seasickness at her kind invitation. Shades of her closeness with Lorelei and up-till-this-moment chilliness toward me. But I agreed to go. Maybe this was my opportunity to get more involved, something I had tried to bring about for many months. And, at the same time, open to the friendship with Cecilia that I hoped for

By the end of the following day, I wished I had listened to my intuition about the invitation a little closer.

Volleyball Game

It was a cold day, and I was still trying to recover from the frigidity as I sat on the bleachers waiting for the game to start. In a red puffy down coat, I must have looked like a giant radish. Still feeling off balance and questioning why Cecilia took a sudden interest in having me around, I pondered why she would invite me. But here I was, at this event, sitting hunched over my knees. The rec center was nearly empty except for the players warming up on the court.

I watched our players run through their rudimental skills. Bump, set, kill. Bump, set, kill. In the haze of repetition, my bored vision caught a glimpse of something out of place. My high school crush walking across the floor from the other side of the gymnasium. It had been two years since I had even laid eyes on him. The direction he took was squarely toward where I sat.

From the moment I set foot in the hospital on my first day of work, my life had divided itself into two halves. The first being childhood, the second being adulthood. The halves never crossed each other's borders. Until that moment. A lumpy, disproportionate, unreal moment. The moment layered in a thin outer coat of pause, followed instantly by panic. Indelible. Bouncing, spinning, surging panic throughout the atoms in my body. Followed by a feverish core of emotion. Every longing thought, every unfulfilled desire, every suppressed fantasy seeking definition. Like emotional atomic fusion, my energy sought escape.

Revived desire overpowering self-control, I lost command of my legs. Jumping up, I ran down the bleachers and out the door. My rational thought absent to the scene.

Outside, I bumbled into my car and tried to breathe. The comfort of the car enclosure allowed my mind's frenzy to subside to mere exaggerated white noise. Still, I couldn't stop the quiver of muscles running from my hands through my arms, and down my legs. Energy, life electricity, surged from head to toe and back. When calm began to return, a new panic replaced it. What just happened? Eventually, embarrassment replaced besieged turmoil, and I slunk home.

Throughout the day, I struggled with unwelcome revival. The out-of-character invitation, the moment of impact, and the aftermath. All dividing themselves into cruel segments of disparate despair. The stupidity that I seemed to forever practice spelled out in front of me. Bump. Set. Kill.

Back at Work

I dreaded going to work on Monday. I was afraid I would have to explain why I left without staying to watch the game. I didn't want to tell anyone about the crush I could never seem to get over nor why I might react the way I did. I didn't understand it myself. How could I explain it to anyone else?

When I saw her on Monday, Cecilia pursed her lips and shot a terse "Left kind of early didn't you?" at me. I dropped my eyes. "Yah, I did," was all I offered. To my relief, she didn't pursue it further. But somewhere deep inside me I knew I'd lost any hope of getting in her good graces. And even more devastating, any renewed hope of ever making a connection with my high school crush was dead before it started. I didn't understand what happened, but I knew I'd done a bad thing. I wanted so much to ask Cecilia what I should do about it, but I didn't quite trust her. I certainly wasn't going to start by sharing my deepest, darkest secrets with her. Trust is a mountain to be climbed step-by-step.

This latest incident only added to my scrambled fray of emotions. I was still reeling from my premature ovarian failure diagnosis. Now, I'd done something really strange, reacted to engorged emotions in a very pained and public way. I found myself trying hard to hold it all together at work. Coming home I would let the tears flow freely. On the abyss that was my life, I was grabbing at a severed edge. On top of that, the headaches flourished with every teardrop I shed.

Meeting My First Angel

"So, why have you come to see me?"

I was sitting in a large comfortable chair across from a psychologist in her office. I'd spent several months feeling blue and fighting to keep from choking up every second of the day. The fact that I thoroughly did not understand why I had done what I did kept taunting me with guilt, despair, hopelessness, and feelings of inadequacy. These feelings chased each other in a kind of whirling vortex. I felt my life swirling around and down an unplugged sink. I didn't know where to turn. I'd finally gone to someone whom I trusted and gotten Louise's name. Now, I was here. I couldn't go back.

"There's something wrong with me. I think I'm crazy," I said forcing each syllable forward. I stopped to breathe. There was a kind of relief to putting words to the darkness of my bewilderment.

She smiled. "Why do you think that?"

I laid out the story of my growing crush in high school and the incident that happened at the volleyball game. As I came to the point where I ran, I couldn't hold my tears in any longer. "It doesn't make sense. It's exactly the opposite of what I would've liked to have done. Only a crazy person would do that."

I stopped talking. Bracing myself for her pronouncement of whatever mental illness I was exhibiting, I could feel the muscles of my body tensing to stone.

There was a slight pause. A hint of a smile lit up her face, her eyes kind, gleaming with the sparkle of compassion. "No, what you did is not crazy."

"What? That can't be normal behavior." I was even more perplexed by her answer. Her relaxed smile gave me some nervous ease. Enough to keep talking.

After a moment's pause, she said, "Have you ever heard of the fight or flight response to stress?"

"No." I couldn't say that I had. Okay, maybe I heard it mentioned before in my high school Psych class. But what did that have to do with me?

"It's a normal human reaction to an intensely stressful situation. Our ancestors required this type of reaction for survival. When faced with a threat, say an attack by a saber-tooth tiger, they had no time to think. Their reaction was either to stay and fight or run. Today, we don't have many occasions to meet up with a wild animal that wants to eat us, but the reaction is still part of our genes."

"But I didn't mean to do it. It just happened before I could stop myself." I still couldn't grasp this concept, but I did remember the sudden terror that hit me a split second before my flight. Its short life ingrained on the diagram of the rest of mine.

"It's an automatic reaction to extreme stress," she said,

her confident face shining.

I sat back in my chair. I had built this young man up in my mind, put him on the *perfect man* pedestal, the Ken to my Barbie. Fought against a longing many years in the making. An overwhelming proliferation of feeling that grew uncontrolled in my spirit. It was starting to make sense in a strange sort of way. This crush and the emotions that accompanied it had become so powerful an enigma that when faced with his sudden appearance without warning, I could do nothing but shrink from the encounter.

"So, I'm not crazy?" I allowed myself to relax a little.

"If you mean, do you have a mental illness? . . . No." She had a full smile on her face now.

I let out a big sigh. So, it didn't signal mental disease. With my other medical problems, it was good to hear that I wouldn't have to face that too. It didn't make what I did any less embarrassing or shameful. I was somewhat relieved that there was a plausible explanation for my behavior. Still, there were unanswered questions. Why me? My friends never did such stupid things.

Fears, Beliefs and Actions

I'd hoped that the whole incident would blow over. Gossip is inevitable. I knew there would be some throughout the hospital since the whole incident took place with so many of my coworkers present. Still, I thought I and my high school crush were the only people who knew about it. To them, I hoped it would look like I had taken a sudden, though awkward, notion to leave.

But I walked around in a hush. Wherever I went, whomever I interacted with, there was a palpable, unseen mist of separation. Even Beatrice, who was so very nice to me all the time, suddenly regarded me with a cool spirit. A self-consciousness. Preparing for some unexpected act. Like I might suddenly jump from her presence and walk away.

One afternoon I was completely bored with my transcription. Winding and rewinding the tapes. Listening to the droll of medical jargon and surgical procedure. The incessant drone wound to a dead space. I reached out with my right hand to flip the tape over while my left hand pulled the nagging earplugs from their work of drowning out external sound. It was then that I heard my name followed by an unkind smear of backstabbing. The slanderous content was clearly about my volleyball blunder.

I looked out the door to our office. It emptied directly into the larger office I used to occupy. Not six feet from its opening was Cecilia's desk. She had her back turned, talking on the phone, but her voice carried clearly into my hearing. While only gleaning one side of the conversation, it was clear that she was talking to my high school crush in a kind of dual put down session.

I listened for a few minutes, each insult jabbing wound after wound into my chest. As she ended the conversation and put the phone back in its cradle, I hastily shoved the headset back in place. Cecilia whipped around in one swift motion. Our eyes met briefly. A shot of venom from one line of sight to the other.

I quickly placed my earphones onto my head, but just in front of my ears so they didn't block my hearing and looked toward my feet as if adjusting the foot peddle. But I didn't start the tape. Cecilia began relaying her phone conversation to her confidante in the desk next to her. I listened while acting as if I were working. She did not lower her voice, as if she dared me to confront her.

They know each other? I thought. *How? What happened after I left?*

Circumstances could not get worse than this.

Confiding in Louise

"I don't think I trust Cecilia," I said opening my next session with Louise.

"Why is that?" was her response.

"I just don't."

Louise regarded me with a pensive look. Her eyes narrowed quizzically. I didn't want to reveal what I had heard. I knew what she would say. How could I be sure they were talking about me? I knew. I just knew. I'd practically heard the entire conversation. Yes, one side of it, but enough to know. Then, Louise would urge me to confront her. I wasn't going to do that. She intimidated me.

"I just don't," I repeated with as much force and vigor as I could bring forward.

After a moment's pause, Louise's eyes grew soft. "Maybe the reason you don't trust her is because you can't trust her. She is not someone worthy of your trust."

That was all I needed to hear. I could trust my own inclinations. I could trust my own feelings. And they told me not to trust. Cecilia. This new validation from someone whose job it was to know about me was enough backing to give me hope. I may be sensitive, but I had just learned that that label of misperception that had followed me throughout my life till now did not mean I couldn't trust myself to discern the true intentions of others. A welcome affirmation of my competency.

Coach

Wyn's eyes grew wide and a smile lit his face. "You're tall. You'll be our center."

I tried to force a smile onto my reflexive grimace. The last place on earth I wanted to end up was here. But the two of them, my mother and Susan, her coworker/friend, had ganged up on me. Susan's younger brother was trying his hand at coaching a women's basketball team. She and my mother had gotten together and decided to recruit me.

My mother was an excellent basketball player. Growing up, she had played in school at a time in history when it was not popular nor even widely accepted that women play sports in school. I did not get her athletic genes, but she seemed to believe that all I needed to do was practice a little and I could be an athlete. And Susan was recruiting for her brother Wyn's team. He was approaching the start of the season and was scrambling for players. If he couldn't recruit one more, there would be no team. I was no match for the two targeted motivations.

I could've held out my "no" longer, but tensions between Cecilia and I were gaining strength. I'd overheard more telephone calls where my name was mentioned. She and I barely spoke. When we did, I guarded my words with fierce resolve, Louise's admonition still in my ears. With these added tensions, I no longer wanted to participate in the hospital's singles' activities. I would have to venture out on my own.

Standing in the doorway at the rec center's gym, my feet attached to the floor, I tried to push my way in. It was the team's night to occupy the gym for practice. He saw me standing at the door and waved me in. The wave hearty, the smile broad and genuine. The ground released my feet.

After practice, he took me aside. "I want to do some one-on-one work with you," he said.

"I know I'm not good at this," I said, "I'm not an athlete."

"You just need practice," he said.

We had several private practice sessions over the next few weeks. He was determined to make me into his star player.

Our relationship may not have been rewarding for him – our team ended the season in last place. But it was for me. I had made my first male friend. Someone who liked me for who I was, a man that I spent time with, but without romantic chemistry on either side. Easing the tension I felt around men in general.

<u>Bridal Shower</u>

The call from Sindy was a surprise but a pleasant one. I hadn't seen or talked to her in probably four or five years. Since our separation to different high schools. She was getting married soon and wanted to know if I would come to her bridal shower. Of course, I wouldn't miss it.

Hanging up, I was thrilled and frightened to my core at the same time. It seemed all my friends were getting married. I was going to one shower and wedding after another. I was even a bride's maid for one or two weddings. But I never expected to hear from Sindy. After the Stacy incident, I was weary that Sindy too had forgotten all about me.

That's where the fear came in. The three of us had been so close in junior high. Then, Stacy and Sindy both went off to the same high school, disappearing into the distance together. I was sure they had maintained and even strengthened their friendship while I dropped out of recall. There was no doubt in my mind that Stacy would be there.

How could I face her? In the time since I'd accidentally run into her in my senior year, I'd contemplated that moment. Trying to understand what had happened. She'd disowned me. That was evident. I'd had my friends remind her of me twice. Each time she either honestly didn't remember me or had made the decision not to know me anymore. I didn't know which was worse. Neither made me happy. Still, the look on her face, the split-second glimpse I'd had when I passed her unacknowledged, had haunted me.

There was recognition in her response. Although not complete. I could see that. More than that, I could feel it. It sunk into my soul, weighing me down. I'd chastised myself, *what an ogre you are.* But the confusion remained.

The chill in that accidental meeting, with its lingering questions, conflicted me. Unaccustomed to confrontation, I'd always dealt with difficult emotional issues by avoiding them.

But in the intimacy of a group of young women at a bridal shower, I was afraid avoiding her would be impossible.

On the afternoon of the shower, my dread had reached its pinnacle. I approached the door to the party with trepidation. I had to go. I refused to let Sindy down by not showing up. The apprehension I felt was strong. It welled in my chest, making a lump in my throat.

As I entered the room and looked around, I did not see one familiar face. Stacy was not here. I exhaled in silent relief and told myself I could stop my worries and enjoy the party. Still the foreboding feeling shadowing me remained. I attributed it to the notion that she could show up at any moment. As the party started and still no Stacy, I tried to relax. But the restlessness remained.

Being in groups of people that I didn't know had started to bother me. I didn't quite understand. I'd gone through school being in large groups of people. There was always apprehension because I didn't know anyone, but this new nervousness was something beyond the shyness of new situations. In groups like this I felt an exhaustion. Mental as well as physical. Like every ounce of my energy was being slowly depleted. Taken from me. Oozing from my body. Leaving like mist spreading outward in all directions.

After the obligatory games, I contemplated making a quick exit. Stacy was not there, had not been there, and was unlikely at this point to show up. I could leave and be happy that I had not had to face her. Still, I stayed. I didn't want to be the first to leave and I didn't want to lose another friend like I had lost in Stacy. I sat in the circle of women who all knew each other, saying nothing, forcing a smile to my face at their banter. The blur of excitable conversations flowing through me in awkward white noise.

What caught my sudden attention was a woman across the room from me. Her mood much more than joyful. She was rapturous in her manner. I listened in on her conversation.

Several other women began to cluster around her as she revealed her ring. She gushed on and on about her recent engagement. She talked fast revealing her excitement, her love. Within mere moments I knew the name of her fiancé.

I had to stifle a reflexive gasp. So, he was engaged. My high school crush was getting married.

If there was anything worse than running into Stacy, it was running into this news. Head on. With no warning. My distress seemed to apex and explode like a fourth of July finale. I didn't understand. He was still calling Cecilia to complain about me. The last time being the Friday before this weekend party. Yesterday. I couldn't rationalize the two components; taking the step to be with someone for the rest of his life and still calling on Cecilia to grumble about me running away from him. Embarrassing him. So many months ago. These two acts together, at the same time, didn't coalesce.

I could sit still no longer. The air became thin. My breath came in short gasps. I felt a crushing feeling around my chest, pushing in on my heart. There was no chance at fighting this command of the heart. I had to get out of there. It was a conscious as well as a subconscious decision. I scrambled to my feet. Sought Sindy out, gave her a hug, wished her the best, and said my goodbyes. I moved with mechanical precision.

When I was free, I fled into the freedom of open air. The breath of clean oxygen. Into the solitude of my car. Alone where I could comprehend the silence. Let it seep into me and cleanse the whirlwind in my soul. Where my thoughts were sound, and I could shut out what was incongruous in my life.

Phantosmia

One afternoon as I worked transcribing medical records, there was a sudden horrible odor in our small office. Powerful and overwhelming, it infiltrated my nostrils. I looked up, and around. There was nothing out of order.

"What is that horrible smell?" I said.

Beatrice, Lorelei and the other three women in the office looked up from their typing. In stunned unison they answered, "What smell?"

My cheeks reddened. It dominated the room, pervasive and vile.

"That awful, foul smell," I continued. Surely, they knew what I was talking about.

I looked from face to face, each head shaking from side to side. "No, I don't smell it." "Me either."

I turned back to my typewriter. The smell had dissipated for me too. Quickly. So much so I wondered how so much of it had escaped so fast. A surreal event in a surreal moment.

For the next five minutes I tried to push it out of my mind and return to my work. But the odor soon returned.

I glanced covertly around the room. Not one of my co-workers seemed distracted or even looked up. I bit my lip and tried to dismiss the smell. Within minutes it had vanished again, not to return that day.

A smell this strong that only I could detect. It was an anomaly I could not ignore. I consulted a doctor who thought it was a sinus infection and gave me a nasal spray.

I Am Not My Father

"I am not my father." The chair in Louise's office got suddenly bumpy and uncomfortable. I shifted in my seat.

"No, you're not.," Louise said. I had recalled a memory that had unsettled me for years. It was a time when my mother and I were at odds. Most mothers and teenage daughters go through a difficult period and we were no exception. Most of those memories had faded away to oblivion, or at least nontoxic coexistence with my other recollections.

This one stuck out and still brought the ire out in me.

During one of our confrontations, she had brought the conflict to an abrupt end with "You're just like your father." Not only had it stopped me in my tracks back then, but it also still hurt years later.

"Where are the tears coming from?" Louise gently prodded. I was lost in an emptiness. Like floating time and space. Black all around me.

"I don't know." I honestly answered her question, coming back to the present. "I don't know."

"Try," she said.

Chapter 3 - Emergence

<u>Gifted Child</u>

Like an elaborate Rube Goldberg machine, my future began with two simultaneous pushes on domino life events. These two events, the disastrous shame that ended any hope for my high school crush and the threshold realization that my life would never resemble my early Game dreams, converged in the moments I started seeing Louise.

I looked forward to our sessions together, hungered for the attention, the self-centered thrill of having a captive audience to share my unreleased emotions. And yet, I hated each session equally once they began. The emotional anguish exhausted me.

The simplicity of acknowledging that my self-esteem suffered very soon hit the wall of complexity for why. In her insightful wisdom, Louise pinpointed what was hidden to me. Hidden but so revealing to who I was.

She started one session with an explanation of what a gifted child was. I was curious but didn't understand why she thought this was important to our discussions. At first, I rejected the "gifted child" tag. There was something unsettling in being called gifted when I had no talent for anything. Louise thought a moment. Perhaps she should explain it another way. I listened.

When my father's pain-filled glare prompted me to turn down any noise and withdraw to my room, when my mother's insistence that I was just like my father shut down any conflict between us, and other similar incidents occurred – I learned to retreat, feelings as well as presence, into silence. A *sensitive* child, otherwise referred to as gifted, Louise would say, learns to adapt and place others' needs way above her own.

These words brought the first sting to my eyes. This insight so affirmative. Learning that my feelings had worth was a long and arduous process that began at that moment.

In the meantime, Louise suggested I read Alice Miller's *Prisoners of Childhood: The Drama of the Gifted Child and the Search for the True Self.* I read the book, finding bits and pieces of me in it. The "inner riches" the book referred to, "great intensity of feeling, depth of experience, curiosity, intelligence, quickness—and … ability to be critical" were the sensitive child's gifts.

Certain of these inner riches felt right on. The pain of my summer friend's broken romance crippling my social growth. Placing that friend's feelings above my own. The inner conflict that arose from the entanglement of the two. Other events in my life. Placing my family's and everyone's feelings above my own. My reticence to even be in the same room as Lorelei, the Swan-Killer, whose joking and laughter delighted so many others but made my skin grow goose bumps. The deep wounds inflicted from my friends' boyfriends' chiding and put-downs. The differences that separated me from so many of my friends. The list went on.

The sensitive child responds to an environment where these gifts are misunderstood, and used, by parents and others, to their own advantage. Causing sensitive "gifted" children to lose sight of their own needs and desires, while placing, as Louise said, others' needs and desires above their own.

Too close to my own experience to disown, I certainly identified with the connections between the characteristics of the gifted child and myself. I was willing to accept part of the theory. The part that told me where I needed work. But I continued to resist the label "gifted."

What it did for me was to pull me from the desperation I'd felt over the preceding months. It revived my hope. Maybe if I worked these weaknesses in my character out, then I could still hold onto the dream, have the life I wanted, be the person I'd dreamed of on my neighbor's porch.

Meditation

My sessions with Louise were the breath that gave me life during my early 20's. She had a way of lifting my spirits like nothing else. Her insights into my life were on target. The relationship with her a craving in my soul. A guide down the path I desired to go but had no clue how to navigate.

She had helpful suggestions for my headaches, but also suggestions to address my anxiety and my increased propensity for the fight-or-flight response, the two so linked. It was through her suggestion that I began meditating twice a day.

The first few years I did "meditation," it was not meditating as I do now. It was more of a progressive relaxation exercise. Silently talking myself through a head-to-toe relaxation of every muscle in my body. This allowed me to hit a sense of calm and total relaxation that I never felt in my life before. After week-after-week and month-after-month of doing this relaxation, I would sit down with the intention of doing it and instantly feel the calm start before I began the mental monologue that went with it.

Through a couple of years of practice, I grew restless and began experimenting with other forms of meditation. But, for now, half an hour in the morning and half an hour before bed sent a muscular peace throughout my body that extended into my waking awareness all day long. With this peace, joy also entered my life.

I still sensed a fear reflex within, but I had taken my first steps toward calming the beast. I chose to look at it as a victory.

Saying Goodbye

I stood in my tiny kitchen, hugging my shoulders. The decision had been made. I was getting ready to make a big change in my life.

With bits of joy breaking through my sadness came

resolve.

I'd spent months listening to Cecilia, my chosen social mentor, talk about my dismal qualities through an open door in the transcription room. When I was supposed to be transcribing the doctors' words through my earphones, I was on double awareness. It would inevitably start with a phone call from which she would emerge agitated. Listening to her talk, I occasionally caught the staccato puncture of my name. After getting off the phone, she would send glaring glances my way while talking to the woman at the desk next to her. Their joined and angry voices soon became recognizable to me, like a flock of angry geese. I initially tried to ignore the drama coming from her desk not six feet from mine, but seeing my name pronounced (my first job as a preteen was teaching lip-reading to a woman losing her hearing) drew my attention back to her conversation. I would stop the foot pedal sending words into my ears and with the earphones slightly ajar I would strain to listen to her latest trash talk on me.

This only added to my guilt. A guilt that I had tried to dissuade with no success. A guilt that weighed so heavily on me that I'd made the most inappropriate gesture to that point of my life. That hideous phone call.

Now I couldn't stay. I had to get out.

I ran my idea past Louise. Move to a larger metropolitan area away from the mid-sized town I grew up in. Start fresh. Away from the hospital and my new reputation as the biggest jerk on the planet. Away from the memory of my high school crush and my shameful behavior.

I had endured others' anger. I had heaped my own anger on top of that. I was now tired of it. Tired of all the anger projected my direction, it was time for a bit of my own.

I fished down into my trash and took out an old tuna can. *This should do nicely,* I tried to smile to myself. I went in search of the newspaper clipping announcing his engagement and a box of matches. Holding these in my hand, I set the tuna can and myself on the hard Formica covered concrete of my kitchen floor. The same floor I, just a week or two earlier, had squatted on impaling myself with barbs, scolding my actions.

I wadded up the clipping and placed it in the tuna can, centered, so it wouldn't escape. I lit a match and set one side, then the other on fire. If I could've thrown the memories, the hope, the confusion, the indecision, the despair on there too, I would've. As it was, I had to settle for the symbolism.

"I cut you out of my life," I whispered to the embers. "I have new adventures to pursue."

The physical pain began to lift, but what remained was an ache of loneliness. Still, I desperately needed this fresh outlook. The edge it created. I needed the oomph. As I forced these new thoughts forward, an authentic smile formed on my face and on my future.

The ritual done, I was ready to move toward that fresh start. I found a different job and I moved away.

Measles and Aura

When I was about eight years old, I got a severe case of measles. I'd already had the typical childhood ones – these were a different strain, a bad one. On a feverish afternoon, I occupied my time by watching little golden globes of light float gently across my field of vision. They would start on the left side and rise in an arc to the midpoint between my eyes, then arc gently back down to the right.

I was mesmerized. I'd never seen such a thing before. Like a day in rapid motion, these miniature sunrise/sunset scenarios would repeat in quick succession one after another. Once my little sun set, I'd see one start again to my left and I would start the process all over again.

After I'd recovered, I'd chalked up the experience to my illness and feverish condition at the time. The incident was soon forgotten and stayed forgotten until one day many years later when the rise/set reappeared. It was a day that I felt normal. Of course, normal for me by now meant the constant presence of a minor-pain headache. These low-grade headaches I came to call my daily headaches.

My miniature suns appeared again, but this time they were set in a background of fuzzy, sparkling highlights. The fuzziness blended to brown and an area of no vision. The sparkles twinkled like Christmas lights traveling at quantum speed. All this framed the arc where the tiny sun globes floated in my line of sight.

As an adult, this concerned me much more than when I was a child fighting a feverish measles-induced vision. But I'd also learned more about migraine by this time. I feared that this was what was called migraine aura. I soon learned I was right.

Commitment to Change

Once I moved, I decided to make a firm commitment to emotional maturity. I realized now just how bad a choice it was to focus all my youthful romantic attentions on one narrow target. The *cutest boy at the prom* syndrome.

No more silly crushes. It was time to have adult relationships. I had glommed onto a whisper of reciprocation from him throughout my high school years. I clung onto that with naive hope to my detriment. I wouldn't even allow another possibility to enter the door. I now realized how doing so kept me from moving forward, sapped my natural development, and robbed me of other positive experiences. By limiting my heart to one unattainable aim, I had let slide a whole array of opportunities for social growth.

No doubt about it, I'd wasted precious time in hope I knew to be hopeless. My high school crush had married, all my friends had married and started to have children. I was yet to have a real relationship. I had a lot of catching up to do if I was ever going to realize what was left of the dream.

From now on I was going to be open to whatever opportunities came my way. This outlook was surprisingly freeing. And bright. Hopeful.

As I opened to the possibilities, I began to find an overflow of interesting men. I even found some of them attractive. Not in that magnetic, lose all track of myself kind of way. But pleasantly appealing. And I found that staying open to all possibilities would help defray any strong feelings that could lead to strong fight or flight reactions.

What was insidiously disappointing however, was my lack of skill interacting with those men.

When I tried to talk, I stumbled over my words. Going blank during conversation as I did in Louise's office when discussing something emotionally difficult. I would remind myself that I was an interesting person with plenty to share. But all to no avail.

Talking wasn't the only problem. Looking them in the eye proved challenging. I could maintain eye contact for two to three seconds before impulsively casting my eyes elsewhere. Leading to more than a blush of red in my cheeks.

Muscle control was impossible too. The more attracted I was to a man, the more my upper lip shook. Uncontrollably. A beacon of noticeability. Forecasting my ineptness in a very physical way.

These attempts at getting to know a love interest fell flat. I had no success. None. My frustration with my behavior was absolute. I hated myself for my failures, which caused me to fumble even more. It was a cycle that sent me tumbling downhill, unable to stop the momentum.

But I was not going to give up. My Game penchant was a driving force alongside a stubborn willed desire to become the person I wanted to be regardless.

And I had a couple things going for me. One, I hadn't yet run into a socially embarrassing fight or flight reaction during my interactions. At least not one so pronounced. I thanked my daily ritual of meditation for that. And two, I had my weekly sessions with Louise. I knew I could recount every nail-biting moment of a new encounter with her.

First Official Migraine

My first official migraine started off like any other daily headache. As part of my commitment to a new me, I began taking night classes at the university close to my work. On this night, I had walked over to the campus after work as always. Class didn't start for another 20 minutes or so. I grabbed a snack from the vending machine and sat down with my books open in front of me.

The headache I'd had all day had already worsened beyond my normal annoyance point. I was having trouble concentrating.

What's worse was that I was not in the mood for class this night. Unusual. The stimulation of expanding knowledge a passion throughout my life, fueling my presence. But this headache squelched even this motivation.

As I sat there trying to study, I felt a shift of the pain, subtle at first, toward one side of my head. As I gathered my books to get to class, the pain had completely shifted to that side. Pounding. Pounding. *How odd*, I thought.

Over the next hour and a half, the pain grew in intensity. Like the slow and methodical churning of a hand drill into wood, the pain writhed its way deeper into my head. At each dismal thump, it sent sharp spurts of pain into my awareness. Paired with roiling waves of nausea. My inclination pushed toward fidgeting, but I fought against it. Each little movement caused each of these actions to intensify. My eyelids grew heavy. Their magnetic pull toward one another difficult to fight. All I wanted to do was go to bed. Looking at the clock I was sure time had ceased to exist, it was stuck in one place.

When class finally let out, I rushed as fast as I could

reasonably move with stabbing pain in my head. Each step pulsated to the rhythm of my feet. At last, I stumbled into my front door, collapsing into bed. Fully clothed and zapped of energy.

The next morning, the headache had shrunk to a miniature of its former self.

Floating

New perceptions began to appear soon after my move. Not only did the migraines first appear, but other unusual perceptions. One such event happened without any warning while I was working.

Sitting at my desk, working on my typewriter, I became suddenly aware of a strange feeling in my hands. The hands changed location without movement. It was as if they were suddenly floating way above my head. I continued to type, but I glanced ever so cautiously toward the keyboard. No, they were still working, fingers rhythmically moving on the keys. My eyes told me that my body maintained its normal position. But my mind continued to sense uplifted hands way above my head.

I had to stop what I was doing. I clasped my hands together and wrung them around and around. The sensation stopped, and my hands once again resided where they were supposed to. I took a deep breath and resumed my work.

I hadn't gotten back to typing long when the sensation returned. I could feel my fingers functioning normally on the keyboard, my 90 plus words per minute still intact, but the oddity of their location left me feeling out of place. Disjointed. Parts of my body separate from the rest of me. I marveled at this feeling. Dismembered while still connected. All at the same time. A deep sense of self in isolation. Its illogical nature assaulting my logic.

Occurrences of this type continued for months, mostly

while I was at work, and mostly when I was typing. After several occurrences, I became fascinated by the sensation, and craved its altered state. There were even times when it didn't occur that I could bring it to mind, and it would start happening again. Almost as if on demand.

As Alice of wonderland fame would say "Curiouser and Curiouser."

My Second Angel

I found it somewhat ironic that I was back in my old hometown. Sitting here waiting to see a doctor, a neurologist, someone who had come to the medical community after I left. Someone with a reputation so impressive that my current family physician had referred me to her.

Still, here I was. When she walked into the examination room, I got an instant sense of calm. She was a warm and friendly person. I was immediately at ease.

We talked about the headaches I had. Daily, and the one that occurred at school. She asked pointed questions. *Where on my head did the headaches appear? Were they one-sided or did they show up on both sides? How did they act?* She described migraine aura. *Did I have anything appear that could resemble aura? When did the aura occur?*

I answered all her questions as best I could. She was confident and knowledgeable.

"I think what we are dealing with here is migraine," she said leaning back somewhat from her attentive position. "But we'll do some tests to confirm that."

I offered a weak smile. No surprise there. I was pretty sure that was going to be the diagnosis. But I wasn't ready for what came next.

"Now," she said, still confident and self-assured. "Do you have any other symptoms we should talk about?"

"Like what?" I was taken aback. From her intense face,

I gathered that she was expecting more.

"Like strange odors, tastes, periods of time when you can't account for what just happened, deja vu moments?"

I was having a deja vu moment right then. But it was not the pure deja vu she was talking about. I was thinking back to my first visit with Louise and how she had instinctively seen right into my life. Known more about it than I did. I took a deep breath.

"Umm, yeah." I recounted my first experience with the bad smell in the transcription room at the hospital when no one else could smell the foul odor. Since that time, I had had several experiences with the acrid smell. I had learned to ignore it. It seemed I was the only one it affected.

"What does it smell like?" she wanted to know. I tried hard to describe it. I could not find the words.

"That's okay," she smiled. "It's indescribable, right?"

"Yes." I felt somewhat vindicated that I couldn't seem to comprehend its properties.

"What else?"

"I have spacy periods." There were times that I noticed, particularly while driving, that I could not recall moving through the previous block or two and was suddenly further down the road than my last awareness.

She was writing feverishly into her file notes. "What else?"

Okay, I was on a roll. I thought I had better talk about the altered state that made me feel so disjointed. "There are times when I am working at my desk and my hands are on the keys, but they feel like they are way above my head. I have to look down at them to make sure they haven't moved."

Once again, the old fears of having lost touch with reality returned. But she seemed unaffected, still writing what seemed like an opus in my now growing medical record.

"Anything else?"

I was exhausted. "No," I knew there were other

anomalies, but I honestly could not think of anything else to tell her at that moment. The mental act of pulling emotion-charged incidents to mind and speaking them out loud was draining.

She gave her hand a rest. Looking straight into my eyes she said, "Migraine is a neurological disease. Often people who experience migraine will also have related symptoms. These symptoms you have described are indicative of temporal lobe seizures."

"Epilepsy?" New panic shot through my spine in electric tingles.

"Well," crinkles appeared in well-defined areas of her face, "technically we call them temporal lobe seizures. Don't worry. If you have them, they are treatable. We'll run a test to find out for sure."

Temporal Lobe Aberration Confirmed

My neurologist was ahead of her field. I could sense that as I continued to see her.

I had gone through testing, an especially uncomfortable test in which the technician had inserted leads that looked twice the size of 22 caliber bullets connected to wires, directly down into both my nostrils. I was then instructed to sit back, relax, and fall asleep. The last of these instructions would have been difficult to do given my circumstances at the time except that I had dutifully followed orders and gotten up very early that morning. An uncomfortable and shallow sleep followed.

Before long, the technician was gently touching my shoulder. I opened my eyes, and she smiled. I apologized for not being able to sleep, and she explained that I must have slept some because the test was done, and she got what she needed.

When I returned to my doctor, she told me that the test had confirmed that I had temporal lobe seizures. She told me she was going to start me on medication for them.

Explanations

The weird neurological stuff was not the only medical issue I was dealing with in my 21st year. It seemed that my female parts didn't want to work right either. The treatment my gynecologist had started me on a couple years prior had worked well for those intervening years. But now changes were required.

I walked into the pharmacy fully expecting to make this a quick trip. The drugstore had my prescription and I assumed it had been filled.

For weeks, I had struggled with extended periods of bleeding. My gynecologist had started me on hormone replacement therapy that worked well until it didn't any longer. Since my move, I'd had periods that increased in duration until I was now having periods that lasted three and a half weeks. They would stop for a few days, then start anew lasting again for three and half weeks. I thought I was finally making up for the periods I never had during my adolescence. My doctor was concerned for possible anemia.

I had tried many remedies including an in-office D&S. My doctor was now moving me from simple estrogen/progesterone to a birth control pill. He hoped that the pill would supply the same type of hormone replacement with the right amount of flow. I was exhausted, due in part to losing so much blood over the last couple of months and in part to the emotional toll it took on me. All I wanted to do was pick up this latest prescription and get home.

I approached the counter and notified the cashier. After getting my name, he crinkled his brow, and called over his shoulder to the man behind him carefully sliding pills into a container.

The pharmacist looked up from his pill counting and into my face. He pushed away from the counter and came toward me smiling. After consultation with the cashier he said,

"We need to follow up with the doctor. There is a problem with the instructions on your prescription."

"A problem?" I said. "What problem?"

"The way the doctor wrote the instructions, you're not protected," was his answer.

A surge of emotion hit me. Rising from the area of my heart, it sprang into my eyes making them wet before I realized the sadness that caused them. The irony of taking the pill had already visited itself on me in my doctor's office. I blinked back the tears with as much fury as I could muster. "What are the instructions?" I said, trying not to let my voice break.

The pharmacist repeated exactly what the doctor had told me earlier in his office.

"Those are the right instructions," I said.

The pharmacist's smile fell off his face. He looked at the cashier who stared back at him blankly. "But you're a young woman. If you take the pill like this, you could get pregnant."

"That's just it," I said, a tear escaping to the outer edge of both eyes. "I can't get pregnant." I was trying very hard not to lose my composure. I hoped I wouldn't have to explain further.

He seemed frozen in perplexed thought. The seconds ticked is slow motion as I tried to breathe. Perplexity, like a gradual wave, morphed his features into recognition. "Okay," he said slowly. "You're taking the pill for hormone replacement purposes then?"

"Yes. " Relief dulled the sting in my eyes. If I only had thought to explain it that way, I wouldn't have had to stand in this eternity of shame at the pharmacy counter.

"Give us five minutes." He was no longer looking at me. The cashier still looked befuddled.

I gave the package a toss to the passenger seat and slumped into the car. Grabbing the wheel with one hand, I let my head fall into the crook of my elbow of the opposite arm. In my car, I no longer tried to hold back the sadness, the anger, the fear. "One in a million." my doctor had told me in his office that day. One in a million chance of this condition happening to someone as young as myself. Why couldn't I have beat the odds in something positive, something desirable, instead of this?

Mongoose

Sixth grade was a hornet's nest of mean. Shy, lanky, taller than anyone but the teacher, only separated me further from my classmates. Awkward and self-conscious, I retreated further inward.

Walking to school one morning, I became aware of two boys who were walking behind me. They began talking rather loudly about me. And not in a very pleasant way. From their conversation, I gathered that they found my appearance to be a disparaging sight. Their words, at first among themselves, grew louder. With the increase in volume, the dialogue changed direction hitting my ears with intentional force. They settled on comparing me to a mongoose and shouted loud enough for me to hear.

"Hey, Monica Mongoose."

I don't know why they chose a mongoose. Maybe it was a play on my name. Maybe it was simply something that sounded like the worst thing you could call someone. I didn't know what a mongoose looked like. But it was clear from what they were saying that it was an ugly critter.

I stiffened to their words, hoping to deflect them from penetrating my ears. I refused to turn around and look at them. Fighting the tears, I succumbed to the insults. I started to walk faster to escape them. As they continued to keep pace with me, I then ran the rest of the way into school.

As I struggled with the health issues and the dismal state of my social life, I began to feel that this incident was a foreshadowing of who I really was. I certainly felt ugly and unworthy. But through the deep sadness and despair, I defiantly reminded myself that even a mongoose has its place in the world. I had to keep trying to find mine.

Chapter 4 - Musicians

Friends of a Friend

Remaining open to new experiences invites you to emerge from the superficial. And into involvement. To that place where you participate in your own life. Relationship is where you jumpstart learning. Even this early in my life, I knew this. Combine new experiences and relationships together, you fast-track personal growth. I don't know if Amy knew how much I needed her spark in my life, but she couldn't have come into it at a more valuable time.

It didn't take long for us to become friends. I had worked at my first job in my new work home, a law firm, for a couple years when Amy started working there too. She immediately sought out my friendship. Amy was a couple years younger than myself, and, like me, taller than the average woman. We both had played the flute throughout our growing up years. Unlike me, she was quite accomplished as a musician, having performed in a renown flute choir. We seemed to have many things in common. With just enough differences to make our friendship interesting.

I liked Amy immensely. She was easy to talk to, and I felt flattered that she wanted to be my friend.

One day, early in our friendship, she was eager to go to lunch with me. I knew something was up. We'd barely sat down when she got right to the point. She wanted to set me up with one of her husband's friends. William was a professional musician who had many single musician friends.

I was hesitant to get fixed up. I'd taken the somewhat conceited view, or maybe it was the fairytale view, that getting set up was just not romantic. Two people thrown together was not a "choice" decision. But as I had difficulty getting dates on my own, I surprised myself by only mildly resisting. Amy was persistent.

On the one hand, I loved music. Having grown up playing an instrument I had gained a thorough esteem and appreciation for it. I knew I would have at least one thing in common with her friends – a shared interest in music.

But on the other hand, I also knew that many women were attracted to musicians. This concerned me. I certainly wasn't looking for someone who had women dripping off them all the time. I cherished the one-on-one, side-by-side, coupling. Amy assured me that her friends weren't into groupies. With more than a little apprehension, I agreed to meet her friend.

Our office holiday party was coming up. Amy said she might bring David to the party. She would have to talk him into it as his father was an attorney who was bitter enemies with the attorney we worked for. A wave of relief swept through me. Maybe I wouldn't have to go through with it; maybe he would not want to come into that kind of situation.

In the stress of our busy office, the holiday party was an anticipated moment. The office was decorated in strings of white light, and the smell of alcohol made its way into every corner, even the copy room. Staff put on their finest. I'd gotten a special deep purple velveteen evening dress that did not represent my usual conservative style just for this event.

As the party progressed, I kept watching for Amy to show up. I'd concluded she had failed to convince her friend and that they would not show up. But just as the party was about to wrap up, Amy, her husband and David all filtered in. I was talking to an attorney in the office that I had a mild attraction for. His eyes were glued about a foot south of mine, and I kept dipping my head trying to catch them in the hope that I could bring them back up to a comfortable level. I turned to look at the trio walking in. Amy had warned me that David was an extremely handsome man. But I wasn't quite prepared for just how strikingly handsome he was. He had movie star looks. And, unlike my coworker, had no aversion to looking me in the eye.

They walked over to me and Amy introduced us. He seemed nice and the four of us talked for a moment, then the three of them decided to leave. I looked around the room. The attorney whose only interest was in my cleavage lost all appeal.

Amy approached me the next day to ask if I was interested in meeting up with David at their home. She was planning a game night.

"Okay," I said a bit apprehensively. He was very attractive. A little too much so. Remembering the fight or flight problem I seemed to have when faced with extreme social stress, I couldn't trust my reactions. It might have been better if I had gone to game night without ever having met him. But I had, and I did feel an attraction. Maybe, I told myself, new experience plus the possibility of relationship was worth the risk of another dismal flight reaction. As I entered the 80's, I had promised myself I would start participating in my own life.

Game Night

I arrived on time to Amy's home and we chatted for a moment. Talking to Amy was never anxiety producing for me. But tonight, my lip wouldn't cooperate, and instead ticked spasmodically. Amy gave me an extended look, then offered me a drink to calm my nerves. Although I was becoming aware of the possibility of alcohol being a possible trigger for a migraine, on this night I chose alcohol.

We waited on David to show up well into the evening. My nerves only seemed to grow more active in anticipation. I drank more. When he finally did arrive and we started playing games, I continued to drink. It was a poor decision.

An hour later, the effects of alcohol hit my senses with a wallop. It was part too much to drink, part massive stress build-up, all overwhelm. I had to do something to counteract this distressing feeling. I got on my feet a little awkwardly.

"You don't look so good," Amy said to me.

"I don't feel well," I said, fighting the rush of innervation exploding within me.

"Why don't you go lie down in our extra room," she said pointing to the spare bedroom.

I closed the door behind me feeling some relief getting into the room by myself. All I needed, I told myself, was a little space then I would return to the living room. The silence, the quiet, the feeling of solitude gave my body its release. I laid down on the bed and began to relax in the comfort of the dark aloneness. A few more minutes, I was sure, would help me return to the gathering.

Before I was able to gather myself, the door opened slightly and in the dim light, I saw someone come in and close the door. It was David. He laid down on the bed beside me, smiled and reached over pulling my glasses from my face. He leaned over me to place them on the table. I tried to breathe.

His hand went to my side and he leaned over and kissed me.

The rush of overwhelm returned in the form of an atom bomb exploding through my insides. From my heart outward. Striking every meridian in my body in one flash effort. I brought my hands to his chest and pushed against him.

"I'm sorry," I said, "I don't feel well. Please . . . I'm sorry."

I couldn't believe what I was doing. But the unnamed feeling within me had a mind of its own. Without a word, he rose from the bed and left pulling the door closed behind him.

I spent as little time as I could in the bedroom, and when I finally returned, David was gone. I'd screwed up again. David, I thought, was not the kind of man to be turned down by a woman. I was sure it was a first for him. I knew I would never see him again.

<u>If at First . . .</u>

"I wish him the best," I said tacking a smile onto the end of my sentence. Amy had just informed me that David was headed to California in hopes of sparking his career. "He wants to make it big and you can only do that by going to California," she'd said.

I thought her interest in seeing me dating one of her friends was over. Surely, after this, Amy would drop her mission to set me up with her friends. But I was wrong. Her next target was her former high school boyfriend, Kevin, another musician.

Instant red flags went up in my mind. The conflict of mind, the guilt I felt for the feelings I had for a friend's ex, and the resulting mess it created had left a painful mark in my heart. I was not ready to go down that path again. I treasured Amy's friendship and did not want to subject either one of us to any strife this situation might bring about. I voiced my concern to her about their past. Her face grew still while I watched her think. It didn't take her long to answer. She assured me that the two of them were friends only and that Kevin had introduced her to William, and she wanted to reciprocate. *New experiences can only happen if you remain open to them.*

"Okay," I said with only minor hesitation, "I'm up for that."

We were to meet William and Kevin at a practice on a Friday evening, and when they were finished, we would go dancing. As the night approached, I had a feeling. Not so much a foreboding, but a distinct something-beyond-apprehension about the evening. That feeling grew worse when half-way there, Amy decided she needed to tell me that they held their practices at a warehouse used by a mercenary magazine.

When we walked in the door, I looked around. There were stacks of magazines lining every shelf, wanted posters and real-looking weaponry scattered about. In the middle was an open space where a group of men holding instruments were standing. Talking, not playing.

"They must be taking a break" I barely heard what Amy had just said. On the other side, I locked eyes with one of the musicians in the group, He was tall with dark, sparkling eyes and a playful smile. My breath retreated into my chest.

He saw me too, and instantly left the group to walk over to us. His eyes intent on mine, he smiled widely, and said, "Hi, I'm Kevin."

Tiny lightning traveled down to my knees making them falter. The same little lightning bolts traveled upward to my rippling upper lip. Not since years earlier when I lay in the grass as a naive teenager, fighting off the urges building toward my friend's boyfriend, had I felt such a sensual pull toward a man. *This might be a good night after all*, I thought.

Smiling, I looked over at Amy. There was a grunt in her breath as she rolled her eyes. "Nooooo," she said, "That's just Dante."

I looked back at Dante trying to hide my disappointment and shrugged my shoulders. He grinned playfully as he turned to walk back to the group.

Amy seemed oblivious to my dismay as we drifted over to some overstuffed shelves. "Kevin's not here. I wonder where he is," she said.

"So, um . . ." I said still looking in Dante's direction. "What's his story?"

"Oh," she eyed me with guarded interest, "he's got a girlfriend."

"Hmmm." Disappointment clung to my breath.

"Let's explore," Amy said, her eyes twinkling.

"I don't think that's a good idea," I said, looking at a rough looking man sitting on a high stool in one corner of the room, obviously not part of the band of musicians who had by now resumed their practice.

When I looked back, Amy was ahead of me walking through the aisles of old magazines. I rushed to catch up to her, feeling a sudden darkness as I sifted through the tunnel of paper. At one break in shelving, my eyes fell on a spindly table with what looked like a gray metal machine gun on it. Above it was a poster tacked to the wall, calling for the overthrow of Libyan leader Muammar Gaddafi. The darkness approached from behind and closed in on me.

"Ah, Amy . . ." I said but didn't finish my sentence when I saw her stop and stare back past me. I turned to look. The ominous looking security guard was standing within feet of us, rigid in stance, staring, eyes narrowed.

"Yeah, let's go back," she said and rushed past me and the guard.

"We're on our way back," I said to the muscled frown as I ran by him.

Back to the security and physical closeness of the band of musicians, I tried to shake the gloomy feeling that surrounded me. The security guard had returned to his chair but continued his vigilant stare our direction.

Can this night get any worse? I thought.

When the practice ended, there was still no Kevin. Amy sent her husband to go call him.

I Just Want to Go Home

I was ready to call it a night. Kevin didn't show to the practice at all. Tired and disappointed, all I wanted to do was go home and go to bed. Instead, we were headed toward a nightclub. Amy's husband and Kevin would be waiting for us.

Kevin was once again missing when we walked up to the table where William sat. Amy was visibly cross. "Where is he?" she said in short staccato beats.

"He'll be here. He's in the john," came her husband's reply.

A minute. Five minutes. Ten minutes. More passed. I was on the edge of telling Amy that we had to admit that I was being stood up and all I wanted to do was go home. Then, he appeared at the table. I wasn't sure what to expect but I was certain this was not it. His gait was uneven. And he took great care to steady it. When he introduced himself, he came a little too close for someone I was meeting for the first time. On the way over, Amy had mentioned he had recently been through a fraternity hazing and had no hair because of it. He appeared to be self-conscious in his demeanor. I couldn't tell if it was because of discomfort due to his appearance not being what it usually was or if it was because he was trying to hide his inebriated state. Or both.

I tried to smile. He started talking, fast. I glanced over at Amy. Her look was tender perplexity, with a tinge of bemusement. *Will this night ever end?* I thought.

After a few short minutes, he excused himself and ran off in the direction of the men's room. Amy sent William after him who returned to tell us that Kevin was not feeling well, and he would be driving him home.

In the car, Amy looked at me. "That's not the real Kevin. I went out with him through high school. I know him, and that's not what he's like. He's a great guy."

"So, what happened?" I was skeptical.

"I think I know."

"I'm listening." I couldn't reconcile the Kevin she described and the Kevin I just met.

"I kinda told him that you were a model. Tall, beautiful. You know . . . I kinda built you up."

"What'd you do that for? I'm a secretary, for heaven's sake." My self-esteem took a small hit as I realized that she felt she had to "build me up" to him. But mostly, I felt disappointment that I hadn't gotten to experience the real Kevin that night. The revelation left me unsettled, my mood cloudy. *No wonder he was acting so strangely.*

<u>On a Whim</u>

Amy spoke no more about setting me up with her friends. Instead, we focused more on doing fun things together. She had a lot of time on her hands because there were many nights, mostly weekends, when her husband was working.

One night she got a playful look in her eye. "William's playing a wedding reception tonight. Let's crash it," she said.

I laughed. "I don't know . . . I don't really do things like that." I was at a crossroads between maintaining my nerdish squeaky-clean image and breaking through it so I wouldn't be perceived as too much of a prude.

"Oh, come on it'll be fun. We'll stay in the back. No one will know." I got a sense that she desperately wanted to go watch her husband play that night.

I smiled. *New life experiences, right?* I thought. I loathed my meekness. All it got me was behind the social eight ball and no closer to the life I wanted. We certainly weren't going to mix with any of the guests, so I surmised it wasn't going to hurt anyone. *Where's the harm?* I thought. "Okay," I grinned, "let's go."

We found a back door to the hall where the wedding reception was. It was dark when we walked in, and the tables in the back were empty. We grabbed a couple of chairs just inside the door. That is when I saw him – Dante, the musician who had flirted with me the night I was to meet Kevin He was on stage with the group William was playing with. In a white tux and tails.

The attraction chemicals in my brain started bubbling. They soon overflowed. My eyes stuck fast to him and they wouldn't let go. He looked so sexy.

When the band took a break, William headed our direction and pulled Amy aside. They talked for a minute. I got a sting in my stomach. Butterflies with spike strips on their wings.

She came back over to me. "William wants you to stop staring at Dante."

The sting in my stomach shot to my knees, deflating my ability to stand. I was sure the heat illuminating my face would light up the darkened hall. *He can see us!? Oh, shit.* We were, after all, way in the back of a darkened hall. In a crowd of people.

Amy stood there a minute studying my face, her eyes intent on mine. My fingers pushed up hard against my lips, I couldn't meet her gaze. "Let's get out of here," she said after a short pause.

"Yes," I said trying to calm my twitching lip and twitching mindset, "let's go."

It was the escape I needed. Neither one of us talked about it the rest of the night.

<u>Shame</u>

Years before, in my pre-teen Barbie days, I stood on my backyard patio with a couple of my friends. It was summertime and we were all in swimsuits. Sindy telling us that her mother and she were going shopping later for her first bra. She talked exuberantly with more than subtle pride about her need for it.

I looked down at my own barely leavened bumps. Something caught in my throat and I involuntarily swallowed. Resolved to be like her, I lowered my shoulders and willed the resulting pressure to push them forward. They barely moved. "I need one too, I think," I said without hesitation.

I don't know what possessed me to say it. Humiliation. A vain attempt at restoring my dishonored womanhood. A desire to be part of her moment. Or all the above. I regretted it the moment it came out.

She turned toward me, and with a voice bordering on scorn, she said, "You don't need one. You're just doing that to make them look bigger."

I would've preferred she'd flattened me with a steam roller. I had already saved her the trouble of chastising me. As it was, I was left standing there fully alive and swimming in my own contempt.

I returned to that same pool of scorn over the next several days after the encounter at the wedding reception as I contemplated my embarrassing behavior. I had made Dante uncomfortable. Uncomfortable enough to send William to tell me to stop it. Certainly not my desire. Damn those attraction molecules. I had given in to them and they had gotten me into trouble. I had to keep a keener watch on them. I wanted to control them, not the other way around.

Now, I was sure he thought me an idiot.

Crowds

My father hated crowds. He complained when faced with a group of strangers. In terse language, he scorned the people around him. There was no tolerance on his part for them. No understanding that they had as much right as he had to be there. We could never stay at, and eventually never went, anywhere where there was a crowd. Even changing church services, and my father really enjoyed church, to the smaller early service rather than the larger regular gathering. Loud noises and too much social interaction made him touchy. My parents had few friends. He had difficulty being around people. So much so that he had a hard time finding gainful employment. He didn't keep a job very long. If it weren't for my mother's teaching job, I'm sure we would've been homeless. When the neighbor kids called him a househusband, I felt a shame so deep I couldn't look into their eyes.

These were the kinds of things about him that made me bristle. As a child, I sat on the other side of his bias. Feeling a closer association with the people he complained about. Growing up I had no understanding of what seemed his strange personality. I had no frame of reference. I felt no commonality.

In my earliest years I was invisible to him. The craving

that developed due to this invisibility was a loneliness so vast, like the loneliness of empty space in the universe, it overtook me. In my childish wisdom I sought only to ignore it. An impossible task. It blanketed my spirit. Palling my ease. Placing a thin layer of distress over every aspect of my life.

At this time in the early 80's, after having lived on my own for a few years, I now had no need of what a close relationship with my father would have brought me. Missing memories of father-daughter activities, talks, hugs that never were seemed an unnecessary ingredient to the life I now lived.

My father chose the distance, I accepted it.

And in defiance I placed myself in crowds. The more people, the better, with no regard to any underlying sensations that might arise. I was not my father, and I intended to prove it to everyone. Especially myself.

Twist of Fate

Several weeks passed since my indiscretion at the wedding reception and it wasn't gnawing at my daily thoughts as it had previously done. I was getting better at overcoming the shame. There was sunshine in my day. The foot-high stack on my desk was piled with neatly typed letters I had just finished transcribing clipped to their files.

I looked up to see Amy bouncing toward me. As she reached the edge of my desk, she leaned over slightly and smiled. There was sly mischief in her voice as she said, "Soooo, Dante broke up with his girlfriend. You interested?"

Stunned, I leaned back in my chair. My heart started a footrace in my chest. The big question that I wanted to pose was "do you think he could be interested in me?" But I didn't want to jinx this moment. Instead, I said "Absolutely. YES."

Taking Risks

The crude synergy I had with men whom I found

attractive was still with me. Stalking my good intentions. I had no magic to overcome it. It was a lumpy, jagged rock whose only smooth destination was through the rushing waters of trial and error. Experience. Mistake after mistake.

It was hearty and strong on the night of my set-up with Dante, a sit-down concert where he was performing on stage with a long standing and very popular band. An unwieldy venue to try and connect with someone. The only way I could talk to him was to sneak backstage during intermission, against the rigid structure of my values. Backstage, a forbidden trespass. A certain confrontation if I was caught. My height singled me out as a person not easily overlooked.

Amy, being my infinitely positive and motivating coach, coaxed me into committing the violation. As I turned the corner around the curtain, I saw him immediately. He saw me. We made our way toward each other. The weight of my trespass combined with the weight of talking to a man I was so drawn to hindered my tongue. Erased my memory banks. I could not think of one word to say to him. What came from my mouth was nonsense. Gibberish pulled from whatever I could see with my eyes and whatever immediate thought that first sight produced. He, apparently also lost in the land of nothing to say, responded only to whatever babble I put forth. The awkward silences loomed in between like snowy white noise. Frozen in place, the only action of notice were two embarrassed smiles.

At last, he spoke on his own, infiltrating our final silence. "I have to get back," he said, "I only have a 5-minute break."

"Okay," I said. Raising a hand up in a half-wave, I turned and left.

The walk back to my seat and into Amy's presence was a state of two extremes. Euphoric high and mortified low. By the time I reached my destination, the low had won and reveled in victory.

I didn't tell Amy, but she must've realized that it didn't go well. Days later, she suggested that we go watch him play at a popular nightclub. I was hesitant. I couldn't be sure after our latest encounter if Dante was really interested in me or not. He had seemed so confidently willing to approach me the first night we met, and antithetically silent on this latest meeting. Without words, I worried that Amy had pushed him into something he wasn't ready for yet.

My reflection of the night had me chastising all my recalled actions. This may have been my second misstep with him, my strike two. But I wasn't ready to give up yet. If I was still at bat, I was still in the game. I accepted her suggestion to try again.

Final Pitch

"Names?" The bouncer looked bored, flipping through pages on his clipboard. We were standing in line at a busy nightclub lined with young people waiting to get in. The street in front of the nightclub had been remodeled years before and acted as an open-air mall. People walked about enjoying the twilight evening. As we reached the beginning of the line, Amy told Clipboard Guy that we were with the band. She gave him our names and we got the go-ahead nod to go on in. No cover charge.

"We get in free." I felt a surge of joy at this small perk. "How great is that?"

Through a kind of external self-awareness, I sensed the man behind us was intently listening to our exchange with the bouncer. My curiosity sparked as we entered the club and he followed us finding a seat at the table next to us. But it shortly waned as my attention returned to the moment. Amy and I started enjoying the atmosphere, talking and listening to the music. My stomach flitted with excitement. The little tambourines that were my nerves felt like they were going to pop through my skin with every shake.

Dante's stage manner sparkled. Flowing to the music. At home on the stage. I hadn't had a chance to really get to know him yet, but during the past many weeks and our short opportunity to talk, I believed him to be what I considered a nice guy. Really nice. And that feeling of something deeper than mere attraction began to grow.

How often do you find good-looking, sexy, talented, and nice guy in one person? I'd only found it once before. I didn't want to mess this one up too.

But I was feeling good. Everyone in the bar seemed to be having a good time. Laughter and the noisy clamor of multiple conversations floated through the air as heavily as the aroma of alcohol in the smoky mist of darkness. People were enjoying themselves. And I was part of it. The joy of the situation overshadowing any crowd apprehension I had.

I moved my gaze from talking with Amy to steal yet another peek at Dante on stage. Tonight, I decided, I would not stare at him. I did not want to do anything to make him uncomfortable. As I turned to look, my eyes met immediately with the gentleman who had followed us into the bar. He had popped up directly in front of our table.

"Would you like to dance?" His smile was confident. Friendly. He looked straight at me.

"Uh, um," I stammered. I never got asked to dance. Never. Just like I never got asked out. And I love to dance. "Yes," I said at the brush of good luck this night seemed to be showing me. *This is turning out to be a fun night,* I thought as I got to my feet.

We hadn't danced very long when I glanced up at the stage. Dante was looking our way. I looked away, not wanting him to think I was staring at him, but instinctively looked back. Something in the way he was looking at us unnerved me. When I looked back, I saw that he had not moved in that split second. Still staring at us. Not just looking at us. He was standing stone still, instrument limp in his hands, gazing at us, seemingly oblivious to his purpose.

Lightning could've struck me then and there and it wouldn't have phased me as much as that stare. So intense was the pain that struck through me at that moment. Heat blasting my face.

"I have to sit down," I said to my hapless dance partner. I left him standing motionless, bewildered look on his face, and dove to my seat.

When the band took a break at intermission, William joined our table, but no Dante. I was glad that Amy asked him where Dante was. I was still too embarrassed to speak. William scowled at me and said, "Getting his job back. He got fired walking off stage."

Strike three.

Band-aid Rip

I looked around the crowded room. Hopeful. It had been weeks since my indiscretion at the night club. Dante never showed up at our table, during the break, nor afterward. I didn't come in contact with him at all. Amy and I drove home in silence. I stared out the window, swallowing hard, trying not to cry. In the weeks since, Amy and I hadn't talked about what happened at all. I was too embarrassed to bring it up.

When Amy had invited me to their party, I hesitated. I had internalized the whole mess of that night, mulling over every minute with a mental whip. I'd concluded that I owed him one big apology, if he would even speak to me. As if she could read my mind, she advised me to forget Dante and pressed me with a cheery, "Come to our party. I promise you'll have fun." The thought that this might be the only moment I had to talk to him popped into my head. If I couldn't rectify my blunder, I could at least tell him I didn't mean to do anything to hurt him. So, I agreed.

Now, I was here. After scanning my surroundings, I didn't see him. The room was full of people I didn't know. I was instantly swallowed by the feeling I'd had in the bedroom with David, but I hadn't had a drink yet. I headed for the kitchen, got a drink and leaned against the kitchen's bar, playing with the glass.

Standing alone, I sighed. I was in no mood to push myself to socialize and Amy was off being a good hostess.

Time passed, an hour easily, and still no Dante. I started contemplating leaving. My mind bubbled with possible excuses for an early exit.

Just as I settled on an excuse to use, the refrigerator door, a mere three feet from me, opened, sending a trickle of coolness my way. I looked left toward the breeze. There I saw a familiar face, staring into the open door. He turned toward me as I looked his way.

"Hey", he smiled, "remember me?" It was Kevin.

"Yes, of course." I smiled at the recognition. "You've got hair."

"Yeah," he stroked the top of his head from front to back in one slow, fingers-separated sweep. I watched the uniformity of each hair fall back into place, framing a distinctively handsome face. "I'm not a cue ball anymore."

I chuckled. Not only was his hair grown out, but he was not in any way impaired. The night-and-day difference waking my attraction molecules and sending them into overdrive. His demeanor was friendly and relaxed.

Dante was lost to me, I was sure. And Kevin was in front of me, looking much more attractive than the night of our botched set-up. My mind working in intention, I willed him to stay. My eyes growing soft, I smiled.

He closed the refrigerator door and leaned against the bar next to me. We started talking. Like old friends. For the first time that night, I was enjoying myself. Any lingering thoughts of Dante drifted away.

When the crowd that trickled into the kitchen became a swarm, we moved to the far corner and sat on the floor. As he was now, he was easy to talk to. A personable guy. His eyes were kind and looked deeply into mine. Intimacy grew quickly in our rapport. He leaned in and kissed me. It felt warm and exciting.

We were the last to leave the party. Parted at the door with a short good-bye. He didn't ask for my number; I didn't offer it. I assured myself, Amy had it, should he want it. I felt a glimmer of hope. Maybe the answer to Dante was to move on quickly. Like a Band-aid you rip so the hurt only lasts seconds instead of going on indefinitely. It wasn't me, but it seemed other people used the tactic to move on from painful romantic encounters. And I liked Kevin. I really did. Had I previously met the same Kevin I had gotten to know this night, Dante might not have become so deeply ingrained in my mind.

When I left the party, my mood had lightened. The winds of Kevin's attention blew my shifting sands of romance away from Dante. The warmth of Kevin's memory fueled my drive home.

More Dashed Hopes

"Has Kevin called you yet?" Amy stood by my desk, hands on her hips. She had witnessed our encounter without saying a word to me until now. But a couple of weeks had passed.

"No," I said, shrugging my shoulders in an exasperated gesture. "I don't understand. I thought we hit it off."

"I don't get it. That's not like him." Her brows showed uncharacteristic lines.

Men don't like me, I thought to myself. I wouldn't tell her that, but I was beginning to see a disconcerting pattern. I'd failed with all three of the friends she tried to set me up with. Maybe it was something I just had to admit to myself. Either that, or he was turned off by my bad breath situation. Lorelei, the swan killer's insinuation from years earlier still lingered in the background of my thoughts. I had to admit. She was mean in her delivery, but it had alerted me to a problem I had to fix if I ever had hope of being close to someone. I reacted by using vast amounts of mouthwash, but never was quite sure if it was enough. I had to fix the problem. Kevin's rejection made that painfully clear.

"I think I'm done trying to date your friends," was all I could say. I didn't want to be negative. She had my best interests at heart. But I had gotten my hopes up too many times with too many hurt feelings. *Musicians had to be a flaky lot.* Hurt sent the thought flying into my head. I quickly recalled it. Some defense that was. They seemed like normal guys. And not just regular guys, but great guys, ones I could see falling for. At least the ones I had met through Amy.

What is wrong with me?

Flying Business Card

I was trying to proofread the document I had just typed when a business card landed squarely in the middle of the paragraph I was reading. Amy had agreed with me that she wouldn't try to set me up again. The time we spent together no longer included the musicians she knew or any of their performances. I had started looking elsewhere for opportunities to meet eligible men. So, the business card was a surprise.

I looked up to see Amy standing there, intent showing through the tiny pores of her face.

"You have to *call him*. He's *not* going to call you."

I looked down at the card expecting to see Kevin's name on it. The card belonged to Dante. Curiosity furrowed my forehead. I looked up again. Amy was gone.

I stared at it with quizzical composure. I was happy with my response to my musician failures. I seemed to bounce back a lot easier with them than I did with my high school crush. I had pushed aside any internal pressure to find someone to date and had relaxed into enjoying my life again. The business card's appearance now brought back all the uneasiness of my ill feelings about my half-witted behavior. Whether I wanted to admit it or not, thoughts of Dante still lingered in my mind.

For whatever reason, Amy had decided I needed to call Dante. Enough so, to make this gesture. I didn't know why she changed her mind about dating her friends, but I wasn't going to question it. I held gold in my hand, in the form of a 2" x 3 ½" card.

I took his card home. Put it on the kitchen counter. Then I moved it to the bedroom. It found its way to the bathroom mirror. I took it down and stared at it. This went on for a week. The cycle wearing a path into my carpet.

I had never asked a man out before. I preferred to think it still worked the other way around. But maybe not for me. This was the early 80's and women's roles were changing. We could, and in a lot of ways were expected to, take charge of our own lives. Including making something happen with a man we were attracted to.

I am strong. I am invincible. I can face anything. The words sifted through my subconscious. Words to boost my fortitude. My dating life was nonexistent. If anything was ever going to happen for me, I had to be the one to step out of my touchy-feely zones and risk large.

I held imaginary conversations in my head. I grasped the card in my fingers trying to pull energy from it. Courage. Confidence. Callous disregard for conventionality. Anything I could use to help me press those numbers on the phone's dial pad. It wasn't just having the audacity to ask a man out, it was Dante. I'd begun to get the same fearfulness to approach him as I had with my high school crush. My fight or flight fears were growing, and I seemed incapable of stopping them.

The madness that was my conflict overcame me one night. *Just get it over with*, I scolded myself. In a moment of temporary insanity, I simply picked up the phone and dialed.

Please don't answer. Please don't answer. Please don't answer. Was my silent mantra, as I instantly regretted my spontaneous deed.

The Call

"Hello."

The sound of his voice reverberated through my thoughts. Wherever it touched, my thoughts drained to empty space. Fear replacing any sane reaction I might produce. The distance between us so sharp, still as close as my eardrum. He was on the phone. With me.

Anxiety exploded into the emptiness. I had to say something. After a moment stretching the distance between us, I told him who I was. He said hello, and the deadly silence reappeared. I searched the air, the empty walls of my intelligence, the storehouse of overused small talk employed by people everywhere to draw the interest of a potential suitor. Words, the essence of communication, migrated en masse leaving nothing but desolation in my mind.

"Ummmmm, so, do you want to go out with me sometime?"

What an idiot! I had gone straight to the point. Not what I wanted to do.

I had planned. I had practiced. All the buildup. The pleasantries I'd carefully laid out so polished in my mind, followed by a sincere apology for the night at the club. All those things exiled to some lost fantasy of smooth synergy between us gone.

"Uh, I have finals this week. Call me next week."

"Okay," I said, with nothing else to say. My old friend fight or flight reveling in its victory. "Good-bye."

I sat staring at the receiver in my hand, my stomach laying in a pool of humiliation spreading throughout my toes. I could feel the sharp edges of embarrassment shoot up my cheeks. Hot and jagged.

My first instinct was to cry but I stifled the tears. Instead, my thoughts came slowly at first, then into a full rush. Bombarding me from every direction. *You fool! You idiot! No wonder you have no dates.*

After I'd finished berating myself for the ridiculous way in which I'd handled the call, I shifted to analyzing where I found myself now. What was I going to do?

His words were sketchy. A mystery to interpret. Lacking in enthusiasm. But more than that. They were flat, reserved, a bit standoffish. There was nothing rude in his response to me, but did I detect a hint of annoyance? It is in the silent aspects of communication that we speak volumes.

I knew him to be a nice person. Very nice. Not the kind to say, "Get lost. I want nothing to do with you." And he certainly wasn't shy – I'd found that out the first time I met him. If I was going by that first impression, he was not afraid to approach me either. So, maybe this was the nice guy's way of losing a woman. A brush-off.

He seemed interested. In the beginning. But maybe he lost some of that interest given the weird history between us and my foible at the night club. I certainly couldn't blame him for that.

I wanted to get together with him. But only if he wanted the same thing. I didn't want to have to talk a guy into wanting to be with me; he had to have at least some interest in me. I didn't want to turn into a stalker. And if he really didn't want anything to do with me, then it was at an end. I would move on. I had experience with that.

It hit me then. I had to leave the choice to him. If he wanted something to happen, he would have to let me know. As unsettled as it felt, I had to let him determine where we would go from here.

As the week progressed, I kicked this thought around trying to decide if it was the right thing to do or not, all the while assuring myself that I had a week to think about it. When the week was up, it felt right. I didn't make that call. I hoped I would hear from him. Weeks passed. Months passed. No call. Nothing.

I was right. It was a brush-off.

Chapter 5 - A Life Off-Kilter

<u>Helter Skelter</u>

When I was just out of high school, I read the book *Helter Skelter*, by Vincent Bugliosi and Curt Gentry. The account of the Tate-LeBianca murders that happened in 1969. Several years past that tragic incident, public awareness was still keen. Knowing that the Manson family murderers were safely locked away did little to ease the climate of subdued fear still simmering just below the national surface.

This book was of interest to me because I had always been fascinated with human nature. I wanted to know what made people do what they do. And, though grisly, the desire to find out what made Charlie Manson inspire this heinous thing, and why the Manson family followers mindlessly committed the dreadful act consumed me. A human nature mystery. Alone in the house, lying on my bed, engrossed in the pages of the horror that was that event, I read. Absorbed as I was, I had little of my normal awareness as to my surroundings.

That awareness exploded when my room fell suddenly into stark darkness, preceded imperceptibly by a shifting noise. The noise happening a nanosecond ahead of the darkness, the only palpable disturbance against the pure quiet of the room. Instinctively, I shrunk from the door and froze collapsed against my mattress in the blackness that now surrounded me.

With the breath sucked out of me, panic circled my nerves. Terror seizing my consciousness, I felt the prickles of body electricity. Alarm filling the void where time existed.

Moments, like hours, I lay frozen. When my breath returned, it punctured the stillness with a wallop "Who's there?" I yelled, still unable to move muscles other than those used by my vocal cords.

No answer. Silence only. Quiet obscurity.

Anger made an appearance next to fear as the thought

that maybe my younger brother was playing a cruel joke on me popped violently into my head. I screamed his name. More silence.

"Turn that light back on right now!" Panic was still present, but my muscles had melted enough to allow me to push up from the mattress' surface. Even more silence.

"Okay, this isn't funny," my tone more pleading than angry now. "Whoever you are better turn the light back on."

With no reply, I began to relax. With the return of my commonsense processes, I thought that surely someone with ill intentions would've made a further move by now.

Gingerly, I got up from the bed and moved toward the light switch. As my hand fingered the wall switch, I realized that it had moved positions from on to off. Someone or something had to have moved it.

In a flash of spontaneous courage, I flipped it back on. My panic began to rise again moving from nerve to nerve up my body, hitting my throat with a sudden surge. My muscles frozen and jittery at the same time.

I peered around the corners of my room's door. No motion. Noiselessness all around me. As if prodded by some interior force, my eyes moved around and down to the floor where a cardboard sign I had had stuck on the wall above the switch lay flat on its face. The yellowed tape still clinging tentatively on its back, more crinkled and tattered tape held fast to the wall.

An exaggerated sigh swept over me as I sucked in a much-needed breath. The sign must've fallen, striking the light switch, turning it off. The explanation sent a blanket of calm through my frayed insides.

Looking back at this incident, I must've looked ridiculous fearing a demon that wasn't there. A stretch of panicked behavior caused by nothing. Still, I could explain reacting as I had to grim possibilities. There was real danger in my mind. That fight or flight, and in this case, freeze thing.

When the light returned, it illuminated more than the room.

When it came to men, the danger was not a life-or-death panic, although it affected me that way. Why? I didn't know. I would turn each interaction over in my head afterwards, reliving the fear coursing through my nerves. I knew that other women had hesitation, something shy of fear but manageable, when it came to men they were attracted to. What made mine so staggering was my own human nature mystery, a very personal one.

Now, in just short of a year, I had had the chance to connect with three very desirable men. Each one rejected me before they even got to know me. I could search every moment spent with them for answers and still come up empty. Okay, I had pushed David away, but it wasn't him I was pushing away. It was a feeling I could not explain. Much more than the ailment of having too much to drink. Kevin and I certainly had a rocky start, but I really thought that we'd gotten past that. I certainly now had to accept that he left me that night with no intention of entering my life again. And Dante, well, what a comical series of events that was. Why it seemed so easy for my friends to connect with someone, anyone, and all my opportunities faded in the mist, eluded me.

Maybe they sensed the difference in me from other women. And wanted no part of it. I knew there was a difference, why shouldn't they? Or maybe it was the fear in me, enormous and difficult to traverse, that they sensed.

<u>Finding Calm</u>

I love to ride my bike. As a child, I could spend hours riding alone. Not just up and down the street, or to a destination, like most folks. I loved riding in circles, like long distance athletes on a running track. My elementary school just a block from my childhood home was a favored spot. Each of the classrooms had outside entrances with a sidewalk ringing the building. You could often find me riding round, and round, and round the building. The aloneness. The solitude. My thoughts and me. Peace filled my lungs like much-needed air. Centered my being. Leading to an almost euphoric sense of calm.

The only rival to the appeasing activity of my bicycle circles was the meditation that I was still doing to try and relieve my headaches. I was becoming proficient at it, often finding a tranquil state of mind I could never ever experience outside of meditation.

I had started doing the meditation because Louise suggested it would help with my headaches. It didn't stop the daily headaches from getting worse nor the far worse migraines from surfacing, now showing up every six to nine months. But I continued with aspiring hope.

What I never expected that it would do for me was to help me begin to throttle the fear of being in the presence of attractive men. Massive as this fear was, I took small steps forward through the serene routine of daily quiet time.

I didn't understand why this was so. It seemed counterintuitive. But I accepted it as it was. Louise encouraged me to continue, and I greatly respected her guidance. If it helped me, I wasn't going to get too hung up on the "whys." Continuing without understanding would have to suffice. For the time-being.

Sabotaging Myself

Self-realization can come quickly like the burst of an incandescent light bulb's filament when the heat of electricity hits it, sending a brilliant arc flash to temporarily blind all in the vicinity. Or it can work its healing effect slowly, like heat slowly infusing molecules of water with energy, causing the particles to move about colliding with one another, to turn their state from solid to vapor. Inflaming slowly for months with no place to land, when the answer came, it appeared in a flash.

Meditation helped me manage my fear, but the problem was more complex. It had hidden compartments. After rooting around its many hallways, I'd finally hit an illuminated passageway.

The duo of holding out for the *perfect* man to fill my fantasy along with my early belief that I might never be like my friends and achieve that dream, had conspired against me. It created in me a response beyond fear, closer to terror. The intimidation forcing my unwanted behavior, pushing away the very thing I desired. My own actions, whether intended or not, whether within my voluntary control or not, leading to disaster of my own making. Derived from the fear I had yet to understand, they resulted in my inability to connect with either my high school crush or Dante.

I had to take control. I had to understand that inability to connect. I had to understand the fear. Difficult as it was, I would have to quash the intensity of my desire before I could achieve it. As counterintuitive as that sounded to me, I knew it was what needed to be done. I was 24 and I needed to consciously subdue my burning concern to find a man to marry. I was missing too much of life focused on one single desire.

I took a revitalized interest in my work. Staying in the same occupation as legal secretary, I found a new job one block over in physical location. The enormity of this change was not simply in my imagination. My present lawyers chided me that I was going to go work for the "silk stocking" attorneys. In my new office, those lawyers chided me with "so you come from the retail district." Despite their chastising, the move lifted my spirits.

It opened my eyes too. The law firm I worked for vied every year with another large firm in town for the title of the largest in our community. One year it was ours, the next theirs. Our space consumed the top four floors of our building.

Expanding my purview of working companions over tenfold. Women I worked with struggled with childcare and husbands, a thought that brought my childhood Game fantasy into reality quickly. Work for them was a dichotomy of trying to manage all their intimate relationships while still trying to develop a life and career for themselves. Pulling the best from every aspect of their lives left them exhausted. For the first time in my life, I was thankful that I retained my freedom. And I set about to make as much of it as I could.

A Chance Encounter

The new job also introduced me to new friends. Vicky was a word processor whose desk was a short distance down the hall from mine. She was fun, with a full-of-life bounce to her very being. An extravert contrast to my introverted personality. We often worked late together. After a stressful stint, we'd find an open bar and decompress together. For our breaks at work, we often went down several floors to the coffee shop and played cards.

One day, she suggested that instead of playing cards, we go a bit further down and check out the art exhibit in the lobby. As we walked around the folding panels hanging heavy with paintings, I glanced past a man who caught the edge of my recognition. I looked back to verify what I thought I saw, but he had disappeared.

"What's the matter?" Vicky said, looking at me intently.

"Nothing," I said, still feeling the force of my forehead draw railroad tracks from hairline to hairline.

"C'mon. There's something." She said, her gaze demanding an answer.

"Okay, uh." I paused trying to decide if I should reveal about what I was thinking. "Is it weird if you still sometimes think about an old high school crush? I could've sworn I just saw him."

She smiled. "No. You always remember your first love."

I hated that I had to remember him. I wanted so badly to forget. All the bad feelings, all the pain, all the years of wasted time.

"Oh, no, no, no. I mean, he and I never even talked. Much, anyway. It was a crush, not a relationship." If I could throw the light of *it couldn't mean that much to me* on it, then maybe it would release its hold on me. All I wanted to do was forget my failures. And go into the future clean and scrubbed of heartbreak. To my disappointment, lingering feelings remained.

She studied my face for a minute before speaking. "Denying it doesn't make it go away."

Emotional Embarrassment

With the simplicity of a Where's Waldo puzzle, the obvious eluded me while sitting directly in front of my nose. Emotion. I was embarrassed by mine. Its power. Its overwhelming nature. So overwhelming, that it frightened me. If it was that scary to me, imagine how I must come across to someone else.

It was not that I wasn't aware of emotion in my life. I was profoundly aware. The greater the emotion, the more I felt attracted to someone, the more personal meaning I ascribed to someone or something, the more fear seemed to grow exponentially. It had a malignant strength to it.

My feelings tended to grow ardent fast. Faster than what I saw in those around me. Fervent as they were, I wasn't willing to give them up entirely. But I had to find a way to harness them. I had to slow them down. The key to my happiness was not in fighting the emotion I felt. It lay in becoming familiar with it, getting to know it, making friends with it, and working with it to navigate the life still in front of me.

In the meantime, my headache problem was growing worse. The daily headaches were constant and often enough to interfere with my activities. I would get a debilitating migraine every six to eight weeks now. This problem was beginning to seriously cut into my life.

Learning Biofeedback

I wasn't quite sure what to expect as I lay in the darkened room, sensors attached to various body parts, reclining uncomfortably in a comfortable chair. For years my headaches had steadily increased in intensity, duration, and frequency. They had gotten so bad that I now had to go directly to bed once they began, and I had begun a new and completely unwelcome symptom – getting sick to my stomach.

That is why I decided to commit to treatment at the headache clinic where I now sat. The treatment plan they presented me with seemed thoroughly engrossing. It consisted of visits with an M.D. who would prescribe medications with the knowledge of the most current forms of treatment, physical therapy two to three times a week, and biofeedback sessions with a psychologist and a trained biofeedback technician.

At this moment, I was having my first biofeedback session. I had gone through a rigorous question and answer session before getting to this point. Now I was instructed to just relax while the technician gathered baseline information.

The psychologist was a white-haired, older gentleman who appeared to be past retirement age, but who loved to chatter on about the benefits of his clinic. According to him, they had had an inordinate amount of success helping people with my condition. He chattered on, in my interview, about the differences between classic and common migraine, and how we had to be very careful to identify mine in the correct way so as not to teach the wrong method of dealing with them.

Evidently, if we made this initial mistake, I would only hurt my cause rather than help it.

I hoped that I had given the answers that led to the right choice of treatment option. There was no room for error – I had to get it right. The truth was that I was angry. The menace migraine had slipped into my life with violent force. As I sat by hopeful that it would simply sputter and die, all it did was gain ground. Now, I was ready for war.

I was bringing the full artillery. The migraines were imposing too much on my life. They had to go.

We began with a relaxation process. Easy enough. I'd done that for years.

"Let's start with your hands," the voice from the other side of the glass said. "Put your attention on your hands."

"Okay," I said. My hands lay one on top of the other in my lap. Their presence snapped to my attention.

"Try to imagine them warming up, like you were placing them over a fire on a cold day."

My powers of daydream were strong. Always had been. Too often, I thought I spent far too long in my mind, rather than in the day-to-day. On this occasion, though, I was more than happy that I had such a diversion because as I produced this scenario, my hands responded to the instruction almost immediately.

I could feel them warm. Tingling sensations began appearing under my skin. Like little jolts of electricity. Pushing upward, forcing warmth throughout my palms and fingers.

"That's what we want," the voice from the other side of the glass said ecstatically, the electrodes having measured positive movement. "Good work."

Too Damn Tall

I found myself sitting in the car's back seat. The vehicle belonged to one of our attorneys. Beside me a secretary from the floor above us. In the front passenger seat was Vicky. Driving was the lone man in the car. Vicky and the other secretary were attracted to the attorney doing the driving. Obviously attracted. We'd all gone out for a drink after work. The lawyer and I had restricted our orders to nonalcoholic choices. Vicky and the woman beside me ordered alcohol. It was now dark and late, and both Vicky and the other woman had had way too much to drink. This fact became apparent when the two of them started a verbal fight over our driver.

Their banter back and forth was painful to listen to. Embarrassing. I wondered if Vicky would remember this in the morning and if regret would follow. The lawyer at the center of the fracas squirmed in his seat and nervously eyed the road ahead of him.

I had gathered my courage and was about to tell the two of them to take opposite corners when our driver turned and looked squarely at me. "I'd ask you out," he said before returning his gaze back to the road, "if you weren't so damn tall."

Vicky and our other passenger stopped their squabble mid-sentence. Our driver returned to his watchful vigilance, eyes straight ahead.

Stunned, I felt a sudden stab in my stomach area. If he wanted to shut them up, he could've found a better way to do it than insult me. I had no control over my height. It had always been somewhat of a sore spot with me, leaving me feeling awkward and clumsy. And bruised. A painful side effect (emotional and otherwise) to having longer legs and arms is that you tend to bang them against doorways and other protrusions made for smaller folks.

I didn't respond. More hurt than angry, I retreated inward as was my custom to try to understand. The comment threw me off guard. It had come out-of-the-blue and surprised me. In the silence that followed, I tried to rationalize the insensitive comment.

Biofeedback and Headaches

"Good," the voice from the other side of the glass said, "you're relaxing just fine."

I had had several biofeedback sessions, all focusing on warming my hands. The response was now almost automatic. Previously, with electrodes pricking my body, relaxing into the unnerving situation proved more difficult when I practiced at home. Many of the sessions since the first were dedicated to getting me to that point. Once I got to the relaxation state, my hands jumped into action. My body's response needed a relaxed state to accomplish its work. I'd come into this session with a determined mindset.

"Now I want you to locate the veins in your temples."

I focused. Moments passed.

"Good," the voice lacked enthusiasm, calm and even. "Can you visualize them?"

"Yes," I said. I not only saw them in my mind, but I also felt their presence just below the surface of my skin.

"Now, I want you to squeeze them together. Visualize them growing smaller."

As I complied with the request, I could feel a tickle, a minute contracting sensation in both temples.

"Excellent, good," the technician said. "How does that feel?"

"Weird," I grinned. "Really strange."

One Concert on the Plaza

The building I worked in consisted of a large single-story structure that housed a bank, and a high-rise attached office building where my law firm resided. The building was L-shaped. Both the entrance to the bank and the entrance to the office portion opened into a large urban park area of terraced brick benches, circling well-taken-care-of plant life. The plaza was a pleasant place to take my lunch to and relax during my mid-day break.

The building often hosted gatherings and entertainment during the noon hour. One spring day, as was often the case, I took my lunch down to the plaza and sat down on one of the benches. I watched as a temporary stage was being assembled under a tent and a band getting instruments out in preparation for a concert.

The spring air, fragrant and crisp, drew me in. I placed my hands on the cool-to-the-touch bench edge behind me and leaned back, lifting my nose into the air, breathing deeply. The rustling of white noise, sensation and light brought my closed eyes back to the environment, and I scanned the scene moving slowly to my left. My eyes halted abruptly when they fell on him.

Walking not more than 40 feet in front of me directly toward the stage was Dante. *What do you know?* I thought to myself as I watched him, without reserve, move toward the stage. It had been a few years since my brush with the musicians and Dante. In a large metropolitan area, I never expected to ever run into him again. But there he was.

He had a focused look on his face and looked straight ahead. I wondered if he saw me too as I detected a hint of self-consciousness in his manner. But he did not turn to look at me. Reaching the stage, he busied himself giving directions, assembling recording equipment, and other actions suggesting he was completely engaged in setting up the coming performance.

As the band began to play, I realized Dante was not part of the performance, and he had disappeared from my sight. Even as I casually tried to locate him, he seemed to have disappeared into the gathering crowd. Or maybe he was hiding out in the shadows and tangles of wiring just behind the stage. I let me breath out in an involuntary sigh.

Wondering if I should try to say "hi," I attempted to get up my courage, while arguing with myself whether it would or would not be too forward to do so. I glanced at my watch and realized my lunch hour was almost over. Maybe it was best not to interrupt him as he was obviously busy. An easy excuse to the fear, mature and strong, returning from the past. Emotional fetters that remained in place.

The following day I returned to the plaza with my lunch. Sitting down in the very same spot as the day before, I looked around. No entertainment today. Nothing going on in the plaza.

I realized then that throughout the morning I had slipped into thoughts of the day before. Melancholy hopes. Over the years I had pushed any thought of him aside. Something surprisingly easy to do. But all it took to upend that ease was to simply place my eyes on his physical presence one time. The unintended reaction was a return of unwelcome longing. I reminded myself that barely one hundred words had ever passed between us.

A wave of sadness fell over me as I reflected on the previous day. I tried to console myself. *It has been a long time. He probably doesn't even remember me.* Still, I couldn't convince away the feeling that he had seen me and that it had unnerved him somehow.

As I got my lunch out and opened the book I planned to read, a sudden inkling, an urge from my subconscious, sent my eyes from the page to an area just to my right. Within that split second, I saw Dante walk toward the corner of the bank. He was alone, with no apparent distractions this time.

At that instant, the fear that gripped me running into my high school crush at the volleyball game returned. In full force. The flight instinct sent my gaze to my feet before I could stop myself. *NO,* I gained a hold on myself, *not this time.* I was tired of squandering the opportunities I had. Even if I made the biggest fool of myself the world had ever seen, I was going to force myself to go up to him and say "hi." What was the worst that could happen?

With the exertion of strong intent, I forced my sight to the corner of the building, resolved on first making eye contact, then getting up and moving toward him. He was gone. I was astonished. The fraction of a second that it took to ignite my courage was infinitesimal. Where had he gone? He hadn't had time to reach either entrance to the bank/office building. He wasn't on the sidewalk. Nor anywhere on the open space of the plaza. I looked about searching for him.

I knew I'd seen him. His likeness was too burned into my memories to mistake. There was no one there. Anywhere close. Gone. The only possible way anyone could've escaped was to immediately turn around and slip behind the edge of the building from where they came.

"Move," I told myself, "Do something. Go find him." The muscles in my legs refused to jump into action.

Instead, I stayed on my bench during the rest of my lunch hour, looking up every few seconds toward the side of the building where I had seen him. He did not return. A flash of anger flared within me. I had to do something about this crazy fear thing I had when it came to men I was romantically attracted to. It was stupid and making me into a rude person too.

Trusting Myself

As part of my treatment at the clinic, I kept a headache journal. I had made small attempts at journaling my headaches before now and had discovered small changes I was beginning to implement on my own. One of those changes was my consumption of alcohol. I discovered that it was a guaranteed path to migraine the next day. Not worth the social benefits it gave me, I no longer drank.

Hopeful to find other lifestyle changes that would give me headache relief, I dove into journaling with high hopes. The diary consisted of a grid sectioned into hours of my waking day. I had to chart how I "felt" headache/pain-wise on the hour. I took note of my moods, troubling or joyous thoughts, stress levels, and other factors. If I needed medication, I charted that as well.

With the notes I took, you would've thought I was working toward the Nobel prize of headache analysis. After several weeks, I took my treasured scrawl into the old psychologist for our weekly meeting.

"So, have you learned anything?" His eyes bore intent on mine.

"Yes." I had made a discovery. And was ecstatic and somewhat proud of what I had uncovered.

"Let's take a look." He pulled the notes from my hands. "Uh-huh, uh-huh." His head was bobbing up and down, but his eyes were empty.

I searched for more in his demeanor. He seemed clueless.

"Show me what you've learned." He shoved the papers back at me.

"Well . . . it's right here." Obvious to me, I looked again at the markings to make sure I wasn't misinterpreting something. "See . . ." I said, pointing to spikes and corresponding jottings. "I need to avoid crying. If I cry, it triggers a migraine." I looked up at him awaiting some sign of an a-ha.

Instead, his eyes narrowed as he drew in his breath. A deepened frown followed.

"You have to be able to cry. Crying is a form of emotional expression. It's healthy to cry."

Stunned by his rebuke, I sat back in my chair. I contemplated what to say next. I was not stupid. I knew expressing my emotions was a healthy endeavor. I hadn't gone to years of therapy to discount any emotion I had. My emotions were a very real part of me, who I was. I respected them enough to allow them expression. But how was I to do that when they returned my respect with pain, retching, and hours robbed from my life?

"I understand it is healthy to cry, but for me it means a migraine. It's a trigger. If I want to avoid a migraine, I need to treat it like a trigger."

"You have to let yourself cry. That's all there is to it. You have to cry when you need to." His voice snapped. He was done with me. Our session was over, and I felt dismissed. But I also still thought that I was onto something. Something he was not willing to acknowledge. Everyone deals with emotion on some level. Not everyone has to deal with a migraine. That basis for understanding was missing in his quick discharge of my hypothesis. I couldn't blame him for that missing knowledge, but I wasn't going to accede to his view either. There had to be some way to express my emotions that didn't involve triggering a migraine.

I would not bring the subject up with him again. Taking my cue from him, I instead stuck to the points already acknowledged by the medical profession. But I still believed in my finding. I kept the link between this expression of emotion and my resulting migraine in the back of my mind.

It's Me, It's Not Me

The church I saw as we drove into the parking lot was small in stature but overpopulated in humanity. There were people everywhere. I took a deep breath.

I was here with Shawna, a friend from work, who had convinced me to join her that morning. Her church was a thriving new congregation with a large singles group. The service itself was alive, the assemblage deeply passionate in their beliefs. Their zeal was infectious. My mood grew warm and uplifted.

After the service finished, we headed straight to the singles Sunday School. I hadn't seen that many single people gathered in one place since the last pep rally I'd attended in high school. Single men and women everywhere.

Shawna was a central figure in the group, popular with everyone. She bounced from clan to clan greeting everyone by name, introducing me as she went. I followed her like I was attached with an invisible cord, trying hard to group names and faces into a meaningful mnemonic for later recall. It was impossible. There were too many.

Before I could smile and say hello, we were off to another group. I was exhausted before getting through half the group. Shawna, with boundless energy, seemed to take no notice. Her laughter and presence pulled me through to the end.

"Well, what do you think?" Shawna was still pulsating as we returned to her car.

"I like it," was all I could say.

"You ready to come back?"

"Yes, I think so." I was a curious mix of excitement and reticence. Glad to be alone with Shawna again, sorry to be gone. Enticing was that there was an assortment of people. And all with core spiritual values like my own. "Yes, yes, of course, I want to come back."

When I reached home, that reticence retreated into my subconscious. Fully aware I was grinning with no one else around, I didn't want to suppress the joy I felt. I enjoyed the thrill of the group but overwhelmed by its size.

Experts Aren't Always Right

Dutifully, I continued sinking my all into everything the headache clinic demanded of me. I meditated – they didn't have to coerce me to do that. Practicing my biofeedback techniques. Going to physical therapy and massage appointments up to three times a week. Keeping my headache diary; this was the hardest to do.

I did not approach the old psychologist again about my

crying conundrum. There seemed to be something missing in his understanding. A lack of comprehension on an emotional basis. But there was nothing I could do about that. It was a problem I'd frequently come across – medical professionals who were in a position of authority about my symptoms with limited ability to help. Either the medical community had not come very far since the beginning of time in appreciating what they were dealing with, or I'd simply run into a lot of incompetents. The neurologist from my hometown was the last doctor who had really helped me.

Despite my reservations, I wasn't ready to give up yet. I was sure I could get something out of this. After all, the old psychologist was full of stories of people he had helped. People that didn't even need all the ancillary services, who had cured their headaches simply by doing biofeedback. I had to admit I was jealous. I, too, wanted to find a one simple answer the way all these other clinic patients did. So, I continued my dogged pursuit of the cure according to this clinic.

"Daily headaches happen as a result of inflammation brought on by migraine. You only get daily headaches when the migraines get out of control." He started this session with me with his customary confident wisdom.

What? I thought. I gathered my courage. "I disagree," I said. "I had daily headaches that started when I was 14, with no sign of migraine until I was 21."

"That's not possible." His face distorted into prune-like wrinkles, a line of red edging his face, eyes growing glassy. "Daily headaches are an inflammatory reaction to migraine. You couldn't have had daily headaches before your first migraine."

I wondered what study or medical science journal told him this gem of conjecture. Again, he was sticking to his own authoritative opinions without considering that there may be another truth. I knew my own experience. He did not. He had no first-hand knowledge. I did. Lost in my thoughts, I wondered if the scientists studying migraine were missing a wealth of knowledge. In their rush to be completely unbiased in their approach to truth, were they all keeping themselves in the dark by refusing to listen to the voice of experience? This doctor certainly was. He had many, many experienced migraineurs coming to him, sharing their experiences. Yet he seemed to stick stubbornly to his own beliefs.

My allegiance was starting to crumble. My faith in the clinic was dying.

Adding Insult

A vital part of my headache clinic package was seeing a medical doctor for the medication part of my treatment.

After a year or so of sinking money and time into the clinic's protocol I was beginning to feel I was wasting both. The old psychologist's unyielding ego was rubbing up against my own insights, irritating my hope.

To add to my declining faith in the program, I made a visit to the MD. He was hard to schedule an appointment with because his practice also included patients separate from the clinic.

This doctor's patients were divided among headache patients suffering from migraine disease and patients whose headaches were due to accident. On this visit to him, he seemed tired and visibly irritated. As I entered the room, he sighed. Looking into his face, a feeling of gloom emanated throughout the room.

We progressed through the first five or so minutes in silence. Shortly after our appointment started and with no prodding nor introduction, he began telling me about the patient he'd seen just before me. In a dull, monotone dialogue he described her in reminiscent fashion. Her pain was intense, constant, and debilitating. He was at a loss as to how to help her.

I sat silent. It was an awkward silence. I'd never had a doctor share this kind of information with me. My immediate thought was that it was inappropriate to do so even though he did not use her name. But I pushed that thought aside. His compassion was so strong. I felt it seep into my heart.

"I know that must be awful for her," I said in full honesty. "I can only imagine how hard it is for you as her physician."

He shook his head side to side. "It's a very sad situation. She will always struggle with this problem. It will never fully go away."

I took a moment to let what he said sink in. As I looked up at him, he continued.

His eyes met mine. "You should feel very lucky. You don't have to deal with what she has to go through on a daily basis." His compassion turning angry with each new word. His eyes piercing mine like rods of steel.

Stunned, I sat back. *Lucky? I'm lucky.* A memory of Cecilia sitting at her desk fuming over the patient whose chronic migraines brought her to stay-after-stay in the hospital came to mind.

I found myself pushing my teeth together until the pressure begged me to stop. My chart was there. In front of him. Chronic daily pain. Illness so bad it was starting to interfere with life activities. An insidious situation that was only getting worse. And he thought I was lucky.

I certainly felt compassion for the other woman and would not want to be in her shoes. But I also didn't want to be in my own in this regard either. I certainly didn't feel lucky.

My own doctor's empathy extended to only one side of his practice. The realization struck in that moment, stark and absolute. It was my breaking point. This clinic no longer had anything to offer me. It was time to start looking for the next step in my climb to wellness. As I left my appointment, I walked past the scheduling receptionist making this my last visit.

Desire to Evolve and Experience

The funny part about having so many people think differently than you do, especially when they are professionals, is that you start to question your own judgment. Particularly when it comes to your health. In the following weeks, I went through a period where I wondered if I had brought the headache scourge on myself. I knew I wasn't making up the pain. Or the illness that went along with it. It was very real. But was there some underlying, subconscious punishment that I was leveling against myself that was manifesting itself in the "trigger" part of my migraines?

Since my introduction to the fight or flight mechanism in Louise's office, I awakened to the life that lay underneath my outside desires. As Carl Jung wrote in the Prologue to his own autobiography, "Everything in the unconscious seeks outward manifestation, and the personality too desires to evolve out of its unconscious conditions and to experience itself," I knew my unconscious was seeking to tell me something. It was not easy trying to listen to its message, like a whisper blended to the quiet whir of white noise.

I had to keep listening, and in the meantime, use the physical world's best-known solutions to continue looking for a way to manage, if not cure, my headaches. It was too important to keep trying to find the answer.

Reserved Enthusiasm

Meanwhile, church and the singles' group were getting more comfortable. I was starting to know more and more people. Faces morphed gently from unknown to friendly over the weeks. Soon, I was greeting people with a reserved enthusiasm.

Social practice was not my only reward. There were

also spiritual aspects to my involvement. The messages in the church services spoke to me. Hope, love, compassion. All qualities I admired and wanted to grow within me. The possibility of miracles. Allowing me to believe in the changes I wanted to make. The lift in my mood helped smooth my temporary headache setback. And quell my impatience.

My Type

I had invited Vicky to this singles' group party, convincing her to join me as I knew Shawna was not going. Going alone was a frightening prospect. I would go alone if I had no one else. I would've forced myself to go. But I really wanted the company. More comfortable at a Sunday morning gathering, I remained skittish at the more social nature of this event. Not only that, but I had developed an eye for one of the men in the group, Cole, a newly divorced newcomer.

The room was crowded with single people, some familiar, others not. I barely stepped into the room when I saw him in a corner talking quietly to one or two others. My eyes hesitated only momentarily.

"I know which one." Vicky's gaze stole me away from scanning the rest of the room.

"Which one what?" She had caught off guard.

"Which one of those guys in the corner that you like."

"Who said I liked anybody?" I wasn't ready to reveal my secret thoughts yet, not even to Vicky.

"Oh, no," she said with her unmistakable inner wisdom. She had a way of reading my most hidden thoughts like no one else, even Louise. "I know your type." It's him, she nodded toward Cole.

I let the breath I'd been holding since we walked in escape. "Am I that transparent?"

"I know you. I'm right, aren't I?"

I stood silent, stealing a glimpse at Cole in the corner.

When I looked back at Vicky, her eyes twinkled into mischief. "You better act quickly. He won't last long."

Teaching

As a child, I always wanted to play *school*. I had my own books and supplies that I kept snugly in an old, hard-sided chest. It was beyond my comprehension as to why none of my playmates ever wanted to play with me. School to me was more fun than most other activities I could think of. Still, not one of my friends ever hungered for the thrill of learning like I did.

Growing up I always assumed that I would follow in my mother's footsteps and become a teacher. My mother had other ideas. She set about determined to talk me out of it. I acquiesced when she eventually told me that they couldn't afford to send me to college. But the desire simmered under my surface.

So, it seemed synchronistic when my church sent out a plea for Sunday School teachers. What better way for me to vicariously experience my long-suppressed career aspiration?

The church had grown so large by this time that each of the Sunday School classes were massive, maxing out most days at around 30-35 students. Such large groups required a team effort.

I was matched with Emily, another single woman around my age. I knew her by face from our singles' group but had not gotten beyond passing acquaintance. We were paired up to teach fifth grade classes together.

Love and Fear

Deep within our subconscious folds are the elements that make us who we are. Some of those elements I was happy about. I cherished my feeling that brought out the care and concern for other people. Even if it made me put my own needs second. I would not trade that empathy for a lesser feeling. I knew this trait allowed me to comprehend a fuller understanding of what made people who they are. A desire that lay at the core of my inner life.

But there also lay traits in me that I despised. At the top of this list was my increased fight or flight response, particularly when faced with a romantic interest. I was beginning – just beginning – to feel more confident around men. I enjoyed their company, and I loved the delicious sensations, sensual and compelling, that I felt in the presence of someone I was attracted to. But as I got more comfortable around most men, I became weary of allowing my feelings to run too high, too soon. The fight or flight proclivity was always there. A whisper to remind me of my failures in the past. And a threat to every new encounter.

This irrational fear of men, those I had developed deeper feelings for, was contrary to my desire for what I really wanted in life – love. Keeping me from its fulfillment.

I had to overcome it. But sheer determination was not effective. I still had more work to do.

Empathy Divided

Teaching fifth graders proved challenging. Emily and I struggled to keep order in our room. Toward the end of class one day, we were trying to finish up an activity that had the kids moving around and being vocal. The kids' intensity level grew with their enthusiasm, building exponentially as each found confidence to be part of the play they experienced. In a park or other open space, it would've been raucous play within a large group of kids. But within a classroom, within a church, it was chaos.

Dangerous chaos as a few of the boys began stacking chairs on top of one another. One youngster jumped up on top of the precarious stack and was about to stand up. Emily and I both gasped as we each saw the future in an inevitable toppling of chairs and broken bones. Emily, closest to the young man reached out and grabbed his arm stopping his progress as he teetered on top of the perilous, about-to-topple mass. With her other hand, she steadied the wobbly chair on which he stood.

"STOP. What do you think you're doing Get down from there right now."

The explosive fury was enough to shatter the bedlam occurring around us. All the kids froze in their tracks. As silence permeated the room, she let go of his arm and turned to me with a look of exasperation. The boy gingerly slumped down off the pile of chairs.

"What've I done?" Her face was purple with exasperation. "I got in that kids' face."

I looked at Emily's pleading eyes. Then I looked at the child as he stood limp, a stark opposite of his former bold self.

My split-second choice came without little forethought. I called the child by name and asked him to come sit down in one of the chairs that remained on the edge of the classroom. He complied without resistance. I bent down on one knee in front of him face-to-face. I spoke with as much calm as I could muster. "Do you know why Emily didn't want you to climb on those chairs?"

His eyes brimming, he looked at me with a tremble in his face and shook his head slowly from side to side. I tried to soften my voice even more. "It's because the chairs are unstable, and you could've fallen and hurt yourself. We don't want to see you get hurt."

The muscles on his face lost some of their grimace. His frown relaxed. "Do you want to get hurt?" I continued. He shook his head *no* with more fervor this time. "Are you going to do that again?" I asked.

"No," he spoke the word.

Our eyes connected with a smile, "Okay, you can go."

I looked back toward Emily. By this time, all the kids

had left. Emily, too, was gone.

I didn't know what prompted me to think that I could reason with an 11-year-old boy, but I was hoping that I had made an impact on him. On the other hand, I felt I had let Emily down. She needed at that moment to know that what she did was to stop a catastrophe from happening. That by grabbing his arm, she kept him and the chairs from imploding together. That even if she reacted loudly, her reaction saved a disaster. I made a split decision for the child instead. Now she was gone and the moment to be that reassurance to her had passed too.

Retreat

I wanted to try and make amends to Emily. It might be after the fact and less meaningful, but I still wanted to let her know that she should not torture herself by second guessing her actions at that moment. My opportunity came the very next weekend. We were both attending a singles retreat put on by the church. Our class would be covered by substitute teachers.

I had been looking forward to this retreat thinking I could get the courage up to talk to Cole. I chastised myself for not pushing myself to talk to him at the party. Vicky's words were still ringing in my ear, *You better act quickly. He won't last long.* I couldn't let this opportunity pass me up.

More important to me at this moment though was making it right with Emily. I set out from the beginning on Friday night to seek her out. She had had a week to contemplate her action, and maybe she had come to her own conclusion that it was all she could do at that moment. But I still felt that I wanted to back her up. I could not get her tortured look out of my mind.

I finally saw her across the big meeting room we had all assembled in. She was sitting next to Cole. They were deep in conversation, oblivious to anyone around them. A sting hit the bottom of my stomach. Maybe tomorrow I reassured myself. Maybe tomorrow I can talk to her. Maybe tomorrow I can talk to him. Maybe this scenario means nothing. As I thought this, I knew that was not the case. Just the way they looked at one another, I knew I would not find them apart all weekend.

I lingered in sadness throughout the retreat. Every time I saw Emily, she was with Cole. Every time I saw Cole, Emily was there. I ended the weekend in dismal failure, not having accomplished either mission I set out to do. I talked to neither one of them. The fear that was a scourge on my life won. Again.

I saw neither Cole nor Emily after that weekend. Not at the singles' group, not at church, not at our shared Sunday School teaching duties.

Stubborn Willed

I hadn't given up on finding an answer to the migraine problem. I continued keeping headache diaries, reading everything I could get my hands on that talked about the latest migraine theory/purported remedies, and trying out every home treatment that did not seem to have an adverse effect. I adopted the premise, *Primum non nocere* – first, do no harm.

I didn't want to exacerbate my condition. But I was steadfast in wanting the migraine affliction out of my life. It interfered too often, and I hated the sickness that accompanied it. Making me hug the toilet seat as I vomited uncontrollably. My urgency to find a solution grew in proportion to the growing frequency and intensity that the migraines brought.

I had met several people (women) who had suffered the same nightmare I was dealing with. All these women I knew would end up in the Emergency Room time after time, where doctors medicated them with powerful chemicals allowing them to struggle through the duration in a poisonous stupor.

I refused to go to the Emergency Room. To me, that

would mean that the migraine had won. Stubborn to the core, I refused to allow that victory. I would wait it out each time determined to find that other way. Migraine was not natural, I was sure. That being the case, all I had to do was find what was causing it. The answer I was sure, lay somewhere in my internal biochemicals, similar in nature to the biochemicals that subverted my will when meeting possible romantic partners. There lay a connection between fight or flight and migraine.

I was working hard to discover the triggers that would inflame the smoldering ember of migraine that flared with unrelenting intensity. If I could squash the triggers, maybe I could control the affliction long enough to eventually write it out of my life.

I was hopeful. Confident, in my belief it could be controlled. Still, I could not escape the unquenchable feeling that the migraine disease was not simply a symptom to be diminished. They were beginning to feel like a companion. A turbulent trait that was as much a part of me as my arm.

Chapter 6 - Perceptions

<u>Hercules' Ring</u>

My first boyfriend was when I was six years old. I really liked him, and he liked me. He liked me so much that he gave me a ring. The relationship ended quickly though when my younger brother took my ring and played "Hercules" with it. From a scene in a cartoon he saw on tv, he donned a cape and stuck the ring in his pocket, drawing it out at the appropriate time to raise it to the sky, let lightning strike it, giving him special powers. The ring was lost or broken; I don't remember which. What I do remember was that that was the last time I felt comfortable around any male who was romantically interested in me.

By this time in my life, the mid to late 80's, I had adopted a new outlook. I tried to look at my experiences philosophically. Especially my failures with men. If I learned something from them, it was worth the pain to go through the experience. Each lesson building upon the others.

With my high school crush, I learned about my exaggerated fight or flight response and that to get comfortable enough with men to have a relationship, I needed to quell it enough to relax around them. Big lesson.

With Dante, I learned that men don't always take the first step. It may have worked that way for my friends. But with me, they just weren't willing to take that risk. There was something about me or what I was doing that made them hesitate. Either that or on the scale they used to make those decisions, my qualities didn't hold enough value to them to take the steps they typically did to get a woman in their lives. I only wished I could figure out which it was. I couldn't leave that question hanging like I did with Dante.

With Cole, I learned I needed to let my feelings be known. If I liked someone, there was always some woman more skilled at interaction with men than I was. And that skill turned to gold for them. I was sorely lacking in that expertise. All I could do was to keep trying and learning from those attempts. One thing I knew for sure was that I was no longer going to sit around and wonder how a guy felt about me. I intended to get to the bottom of it. And move on when necessary. I was still behind in the Game in which I should've caught up by now.

Above all, with every one of these failures, I learned that fear was holding me back. If I wanted the power of the Hercules ring, I would have to take it out and allow lightning to strike it. Doing so would take not only courage but a better understanding of what I was dealing with. I had to understand where that fear was coming from, so I could confront it head on.

If Graffiti Could Talk

It's odd how one minute you are going about minding your own business, confident that you have analyzed every puzzle in your life to its barest validity, when another piece of information jumps up and bites your truth in its most vulnerable spot – making you question the conclusions you have so carefully built.

Going about my Saturday morning chores, I turned the TV on to an independent station that played music videos on weekend mornings. It was background noise, nothing more. With my attention mostly on my normal cleaning routine, I caught a phrase from the station's announcer, "local band day."

I hadn't thought about Dante much at all since shortly after I'd seen him on the plaza, but his memory now slipped gently into my mind. With a small smile, I sat down on the couch to watch for a few minutes. Having not seen him or anyone else I knew for several videos I was about to go back to my chores when the next video started. There were two faces on this one that I recognized. They were Amy's now ex-husband, William, and Dante. A portrait of him frozen to the moment we first met.

I looked at him. The old attraction hormones were still working. I could feel the chemistry that I thought I had successfully buried. It sent its roots running through my veins and up into my eyes creating the invisible glue that kept me staring at the screen.

The band was performing in front of a backdrop – a wide-slatted fence that had graffiti written on it. Three distinct markings across the length of the fence. The two on either side were meaningless to me, blurring to obscurity. It was the middle one that broke my eyes' hold on Dante's handsome outline.

One word – MONICA. A sudden shot of lightening flared up the nerves in my back and into my neck. I sat back in my seat. A gasp within me surged from my middle section up to and through my throat into my eyes, followed by an involuntary swallow. At the same time, my stomach dropped helplessly to my toes. My mouth fell open. Bewilderment and extreme sadness fought for dominance while every possible emotion in between made an appearance.

I had one fully formed thought – *What is my name doing up there?*

Staring at the screen for the length of half the song, I realized that it wasn't an optical illusion. I was not hallucinating. My name was painted on the fence.

Unable to comprehend the moment, I wanted to shut it out. The surge of emotion too great for me, I got up and turned off the TV.

Trying to resume my work, my attention returned again and again to the graffiti. Was it me written on the wall, or was it someone else? Or a fluke?

Had I totally misread his behavior years before? What I saw as disinterest, was it something so much more than mere interest? A paradigm of rejection shattered. Or not. I couldn't tell. All I knew at that moment was it was a coincidence that my mind turned into anguish for long-lost hope.

I struggled to gain perspective. Perhaps one of the other band members had created the prop with another Monica in mind. This airy thought lingered, then vanished like a wispy cloud.

If only that graffiti could talk. Tell me more than a single word taunting me from the television screen. No answers. Just a deep and distressing question hanging in oblivion.

Objects at a Distance

How we see the complexities of our lives is like how we view an object. Close in proximity, an object appears larger. Further away it shrinks. A longer distance away, it become tiny. But you still know the object, what it is, how it shows itself. And you adjust your perception of it to fit your current mindset. Close up, that object may reveal itself in a way that seems clear. Its properties set, no question as to how it presents itself. You know what that object is.

But once that object moves off into the distance, far into the past, it can grow muted. Losing its original detail. Taunting you to pull it closer for a revised look. Especially if you pay attention to the questions its new softened image arouses.

Most people are content to leave their vision at some comfortable distance. Leaving its first impression to carefully hold challenges unanswered. Especially when it comes to issues that they do not consider important or don't want to face.

I don't advocate pulling up the past willy-nilly. It is important to live in the now. But for the brave scrutinizers who delve into the depths of a far-off object, pulling it closer for meticulous inspection, it can communicate a new understanding. The details you discover might even shake your beliefs to their core.

The fear issue with men was a far distant item that I found hard to reach. I so longed to examine its components, leading to a fuller understanding. I had a sense that my examination was muddy. I could only see from my own perspective. What did that fear look like from the other side? If I could comprehend what my fear looked like to the man experiencing it, maybe I could wipe away some of the mud.

I had a very strong sense, an empathic surge that gave me some insight into that double-edged slice on my perspective. It was a sense of pain, vague as it was, that emulated from the other side of the equation. A painful mix of disappointment, perplexity, tinged with anger. Although I had never, to that point, had a man say to me, "You hurt me," I knew within my own comprehension of human nature that men had feelings too. It was easy to deny this to myself, when it came to the men I encountered, because I had so little confidence in myself. I assumed since I knew me to be unworthy, they also believed me to be so. I could easily dismiss them as uninterested. And, therefore, glad to be rid of me. There was no hurt in this equation, other than my own.

But what if I was wrong? Introducing this possibility into my mind presented a problem that eroded the carefully manicured landscape of my perceptions. It was in complete opposition to how I felt. A contradiction of ideology. My beliefs about men were no longer on the continuum of distance viewing. They became like two magnets with like poles placed near each other. The two views repelled each other.

Was I wrong about Dante? What seemed like aloofness in his response to my asking him out – was it so? What Amy had said about him when she gave me his number held new meaning now. "You have to call him. He's not going to call you." I had never questioned why – just accepted that as the way it was. An axiom of the situation. I did not mean enough to him to make the effort. Now, I wondered, was there another reason?

The day after seeing him in the plaza, did he disappear because I looked away? My own reaction in situations like that was strong evidence to support that. And, if so, that opened the possibility that he had come there for the sole purpose of seeing me. And left when I turned away.

Was it because he had entered the same kind of intimidation zone? Had he, like me, fallen under the spell of fight or flight fear in much the same way as I did?

If that were true, it would mean that I had meant something different to him than I had thought at the time. Something more than a passing glance. Something he was never able to express. Something that came across as disinterest, to me, but was as powerful or more to him as the rush of emotion I felt years earlier for him?

My conflict of mind was unsettling. Hiding behind the thought that he did not care about me gave me a comfortable solution, one I was accustomed to. But this new thought put me in new territory emotionally. And played havoc with my feelings. I felt a sudden surge of renewed, and stronger than before, feeling toward him. And I felt sadness at its deepest level that this thought had never occurred to me before. Maybe I would have acted differently after the phone call to end it all. My actions could cause the kind of emotional pain that I had experienced, something I never want to impose on anyone else.

I could no longer, in good conscience, go on believing that I was unattractive to every attractive man I ran into. Even when it seemed that way to me. I had to open myself up to the possibility that that premise was untrue. But it still felt so true. And my feelings were strong, bitterly so. Those feelings fought hand-to-hand combat with the empathic feelings that were equally strong. Like the magnets with facing like poles, they couldn't co-exist in the same space.

I had to adjust to the unbending laws of the universe.

One had to go. I had to set about changing this life-long belief. It was imperative, not only to my own wellbeing, but to others' feelings. The impact of misinterpreted actions.

Joining a Small Group

With Cole out of the picture, I was in no hurry to consciously put another heartbreaker in my life. Mentally, I wished him well. Wished them both well. They seemed like a "nice couple." In a wave of spiritual growth, I wished every past romantic interest well, including whomever they were involved with. Dante included.

As I did so, I hoped that I could move into a space where I might also be so lucky. But not just yet – I had to retreat awhile from the pain of loss. I couldn't call it rejection, although it seemed that way. I had no word for it, just a vague and aching loneliness. A need to be by myself. All I wanted to do was to exist for a while, heal within, and build momentum to get out there and try again.

My church singles group had started a program where, if you signed up, you would be put into the pool of people who wanted to be part of a small group.

These groups would meet on a regular basis for study, meals, or entertainment. I embraced the idea of being part of a small group of friends. It was much more intimate and less scary getting to know people without the added stress of a crowd surrounding me.

Our group consisted of five men and four women. Two of the women I had already gotten to know and become close to. I considered them friends. I didn't want to go into this small group thing looking for a date, only friends.

Companionship

I really enjoyed the friends-only feel of our small group. I felt a part of something. I always wondered why parents of young teenagers encouraged them to do "group dating." I now understood. While what we were doing was not dating, it allowed a group of us to rely on one another for companionship. We all accepted one another, and no one was left out.

My confidence grew as well as my comfort level around men. I certainly wasn't as fearful as I had been a few years earlier Each gathering I went to added to my relaxation and ability to just be myself.

A Companion of a Different Sort

I had a new problem. Or maybe just an exacerbation of an old problem. The headaches I had were getting worse. At times so bad that I would have to miss out on social events. The intensity of pain went up as well as the incidence of getting sick to my stomach.

I had a growing fear that the uncontrollable nature of my headaches would overtake me, swallowing me into an abyss of pain and torment. This larger fear sprouted other fears. Would it also interfere with my chance at forming a relationship? Who wants to be with someone who is dealing with that all the time? I remembered how much I longed to escape my father's presence during his bouts of illness. I was still struggling with the bad breath issue and saw this as one more obstacle to finding someone to share my life with.

I decided to give traditional health care yet another try. I started going to the other headache clinic in town. This one was run by a doctor with an amazing reputation for helping people with very difficult migraine disease.

A Date with a Friend

Simon was in my small group. I knew he was interested in me from the moment we met. There was something different in the way he looked at me. I was not surprised when he called me one evening and asked me out on a date.

I liked Simon immensely. He was kind – a gentle man. He was very giving too. When I moved from one apartment to another, he was the first to volunteer his help and his vehicle for the move. He was everything I could have wanted in a man.

The problem was that while I liked him a lot, I did not feel the attraction chemicals. There was no sensual pull. But because I appreciated all he could offer a woman, I agreed to go. *Who knows*, I thought, *maybe I just need time for the biochemical spark to show itself.*

He took me to a beautiful restaurant for dinner. The evening started out great.

I could sense he was a little nervous at first. But he seemed to relax as we sat down. As we waited for our food to arrive, he began asking me questions about myself. Typical date stuff. I answered, sharing about myself. So good so far.

But I soon became uneasy. The trouble started when I asked him to tell me more about himself. He did not answer me directly. Instead, he steered the conversation back to me. Asking me more about myself.

This went on all during our date. He was insistent that I talk about myself. He wanted to hear about me. Without a comparable discussion of him as the subject. This made me very self-conscious. The attention was flattering, but I was uncomfortable constantly being in the spotlight. And I wanted to know more about him. The unevenness of this give-and-take in getting to know someone left me feeling awkward. Like he had placed me on some symbolic pedestal. I knew I could never live up to that.

When the night was over, we both knew this would be our one and only date. We parted as friends.

I really hoped that I could parlay the "Wyn" feeling I had with him into something more. But I realized that there was something vital missing. I would never be happy, and it would be unfair to him, to move further along when I knew there would always be something missing.

Even though this friendship did not grow into something more, I wasn't ready to give up on another combination friend/lover relationship.

Meds

Keeping open to new headache therapies had to go along with my return to traditional medical treatment. Doctors used chemicals to treat their patients. And I respected my new doctor who was on the cutting edge of the latest insights into migraine relief. When he put me on beta blockers and calcium channel blockers, I was hopeful for the possibilities. These drugs were typically used for heart problems. I had no issue with my heart that would necessitate taking them. But the common knowledge at that time was that in migraineurs, their blood vessels constricted as a reaction to a trigger. Different people responded differently, but I was told that my headaches were "letdown" headaches. When the trigger occurred, my blood vessels reacted by constricting. When the event passed, usually two to three days, then my blood vessels would do the opposite – dilate. It was this dilation that caused the migraine to occur and the pain to attack.

These drugs were believed to help prevent the willy-nilly nature of my blood vessels and provide a level of stability. The problem, my doctor warned me, was that I might see some weight gain with this type of treatment.

It seemed my only hope at that moment. I had to risk it.

A Different Dream

Nearly into my 30's now, my childhood plan for how I wanted life to unfold was gone. It was time to put together a different strategy. My thoughts turned back to school. My first few attempts at going back to college were failures. After my first year at fashion design school, I'd come through the school with some interesting memories but no hope that my education there would get my foot in the fashion industry doorway. After my attempt to return to school at the downtown university, I'd realized that I could get my early credits by going at night. But the 300 and 400 level courses were only offered during the day. I couldn't quit my day job because I had to support myself.

There had to be a better way. My desire to get a career I was happy with had crescendoed. I was a good secretary, or what was fast becoming called administrative assistant. Still, it left me at a dead-end. There was no career path after that. But I needed a degree to move upward in business.

Chapter 7 - A Long-Term Relationship

Eyes

Eyes are the voice of the lover.

After several years in the church singles' group, I was beginning to feel stale. That desire to meet some new faces is what brought me to another church's singles' group. I took a seat in the second row. It wasn't long before my gaze detection awareness started sending warning signals to my brain. The stare you can't see grabbed my attention shortly after we finished singing and the speaker began to talk. Ever conscious of being rude, I didn't want to look behind me. I tried to wring it from my awareness. It charged hard into my perception and would not let go.

As nonchalantly as I could, I lowered my head and glanced backward. I saw the source of my discomfort. He *was* staring at me. I didn't know him. I had never seen him before. Not outstandingly handsome, not unattractive. Not someone I felt a first glance attraction to either. Having relieved my curiosity, I turned back to the speaker.

Afterward, when the social part of the evening started, the energy and noise was particularly rousing. More than I wanted to deal with. I headed for the door. Showing up quickly at my elbow, this stranger said hello and introduced himself to me. Mark.

Anxious to be polite, I smiled and said, "hello." We talked briefly. My mannerly obligation satisfied; I offered an "It was nice to meet you." He traveled parallel to me as I continued walking through the hall and out toward my car. The heaviness of the clamorous room I'd just left was still clinging to me like rainforest overgrowth. I was anxious to get home. Just before I reached the last door, he jumped in front of me. "Can I call you?" he asked.

I hesitated long enough to fathom my options. I barely

knew him, but his smile was genuine and his manner easy and comfortable. He was here at church asking women he barely knew out. One point I couldn't decide whether spoke well or not of him. So many men I'd met at either singles' group didn't seem to want to budge beyond a passing acquaintance with me. After noting it wasn't a bar he'd been trolling, I put another figurative point in his favor. But what sealed my decision was that he looked directly into my eyes. And I found I could look into his without the fear I was accustomed to feeling.

"Okay," I said, and wrote down my name and number.

Setting Fires

Mark and I began dating. He seemed comfortable enough to talk to, and I enjoyed spending time with him. I have always heard that love is friendship set on fire. I clung to the hope that I could find the "Wyn" factor and I would find a man whose friendship would eventually turn into a fire. Maybe I could avoid the fight or flight issue if the feelings grew gradually rather than hitting me all at once.

He wore cowboy boots with an inch and a half hell during our first few months together. This impressed me. Even though he needed the heel to bring his eyes level with mine, he still wanted to call on me. I was even more impressed when he went back to athletic shoes with nearly no heel. I was not too damn tall for this guy.

Tall Differences

Being tall was always coming up. In conversations. In comparisons. In elevators. I entered one elevator early in my tenure at the silk-stocking lawyers' office. It was a day when I was wearing flats. I started my career in heels, but decided the discomfort was not worth it and switched to dress flats by this time. It struck me the moment I entered and could see the tops of the heads of everyone in our tiny enclosure. They were all men. I counted, eleven of them, all shorter than myself. As I looked over all the heads lower than myself, it struck me just how really unusual it was to be a tall woman.

My second elevator incident happened sometime after that. I got on to one other rider – a gentleman who looked at me from feet to head, and back down again. "They sure grow them tall here, don't they?"

"Excuse me?" I said a little bewildered.

He introduced himself to me and told me he was a pro hockey player from Canada. Then he repeated his question/comment to me.

I wasn't quite sure how to respond. If he was flirting with me, it came across more as an insult than an opening. If he was simply trying to start a conversation, he would've piqued my interest more if he'd stayed away from the already-pointed-out-too-often-feature of my height.

As it was, my floor arrived at that moment. "Uh, yes they do," I said as nicely as I could as the door between us slid shut.

Most of the people who pointed out my height were men. But once when I was attending classes at night, I ran into another tall woman. She started a conversation with me about the effects of being tall. Being another tall woman, she had some of the same issues and problems that go along with being taller than most of our counterparts. She asked me if I was single, and I said that I was. Then, she asked if my height had interfered with my dating life. Of course, the answer to that was a resounding yes.

She looked at me and smiled sympathetically. "Here," she said digging into her purse. "Try this group. I think you'll find it much easier to meet men who aren't intimidated by you."

I looked at the card she handed me. It was a singles' group for tall people. Height requirements were strictly enforced. Woman had to be at least 5'10" and men had to be a minimum of 6'2". I was intrigued and stored the card away.

<u>Another M Word</u>

Just a few short years before meeting Mark and sliding into my first real long-term relationship, an article in *Newsweek* entitled "The Marriage Crunch" sent chills through what few single friends I had, me included. It warned women of the statistics facing those who delayed finding a marriage partner. The older I became, the icier and more callous the walls of my single status felt. I was in my early thirties when I met Mark.

After two years of dating, I was restless. Mark puttered through our relationship melting with the status quo. I didn't know if I really wanted to marry him or not. But I wanted to know where he stood. I was in my mid 30's and feeling the death knell of my chance to get married approach. I wanted to be married. I wasn't as enthusiastic for it as I was on Sindy's porch. But the desire was still there. And as far as I knew, each one of my childhood friends was living the peaceful, serene and happy life of a married woman. If our relationship was not headed in that direction, then we should decide whether we wanted the same conclusion.

I waited to approach the subject until we were in his home where he was most comfortable. A lazy Saturday afternoon when we had no other plans.

"What do you think about marriage?" I said, conscious of the fidget in my left leg. A bad habit begun long before I knew what bad habits were.

"Huh?" he looked up at me from some device he was disassembling. Some sort of household item spread over the kitchen table.

"Do you ever think about getting married?" I could feel my voice grow stronger.

He didn't answer my question. Instead, he began talking about what he was doing at that moment while he continued working on his repair job.

I retreated inward, a trait that I found myself doing more and more. Quiet, lost in my own thoughts. I had a vague sense that Mark was continuing to talk to me, different subjects, all mundane. His reaction lending a chill to my interior dialogue. When he fell silent and appeared to be focused again on the device he was trying to fix, I stood up and moved to his bedroom. I hoped to find the solace of a quiet room. Sitting on the edge of the bed, I contemplated any future with or without him I might have.

In the moments that followed, I realized that I loved him, but I wasn't in love with him. He just didn't fit what I wanted. Too many missing pieces. And maybe I didn't fit what he wanted, given his reaction.

After a short time, he walked into the bedroom and sat down beside me. He took my hand, "What's wrong?"

"Just thinking." There really wasn't anything wrong. I surprised myself that I was not angry or upset. I'd just discovered an interesting truth. I was not willing to take the first relationship that came along just so I could be married. The Game was losing its grip.

He gave me a puzzled look. Then squeezed my hand and said, "Okay, let's get married, if that's what you want."

I hesitated only long enough to think how to be tactful in my answer.

"No," I said, "I'm not ready to get married right now either. Things are okay the way they are."

He seemed pleased with my answer and left the room. I stayed, sitting on the bed, enjoying a new sense of flexibility. I felt uplifted to shed the invisible ties of long ago demands.

Milestones

Mark and I had a few good years while I was going to school. I'd found a program geared specifically toward working adults. With my previous credit and being able to get all the classes I needed to graduate one right after the other, I finished my undergraduate degree in three years. Having a degree in business focusing on finance and economics, I thought I would have no trouble finding a good job. I was willing to start at the bottom and go up from there. But I found I was too old for entry level jobs.

Even though I was having trouble finding suitable work outside the administrative realm, I felt different. It was as if a part of me had been previously missing. For the first time in my life, I felt complete in and of myself. If I had to, I could spend the rest of my life being single and I would be happy.

I felt like I had reached a milestone. A growth milestone. And I began to celebrate the fact that I didn't have a biological clock ticking me into desperation. Acceptance of my life as was. I could focus now on other areas of who I was and who I wanted to be.

Meeting Momma

Mark and I were about five years into our relationship when he decided to take me to Florida on vacation with him. We'd taken a few weekend trips together, but this was going to be for an entire week. Not only that but part of the trip included staying at his parents' home.. They had retired there several years earlier.

I knew this was a big test for us. We'd never spent this much time together all at once. He wasn't concerned. I was a nervous wreck.

About a week before our flight, Mark suggested that I gather some recipes together to take with us so I could cook one or two nights while we were there. It seemed to me like an odd suggestion. Walking into his parents' house and taking over the kitchen. Helping with kitchen chores absolutely, taking over very rude. But I enjoyed cooking and had no problem cooking for other people. If they didn't mind, I didn't mind. Still, the fact that he had made such a strong suggestion to me left me feeling anxious. It felt like an omen.

On the flight out, Mark casually mentioned to me that his mother didn't like his sister-in-law, Jessica, very much. Mark's brother, Len, and his wife had four children, so I knew their union was more than a few years old.

"Why doesn't she like her?" This piece of information taking on grave importance to me, I had to know.

Mark laughed. "She's married to her son," he said with little recognition to how lacking the explanation sounded.

I was floored. "Is that all?"

"My mother is protective of her boys," he said, with no reservation and a little smile.

"What about your sisters?" He had two sisters.

"They don't get along with Mom," was all he said. Then turned back to his magazine signaling an end to the conversation.

I stepped up from jangled nerves to something akin to dread. Pulling out my recipe cards from my purse, I stared blankly at them. The words blurred and unrecognizable, my mind working only on processing what he just said.

It didn't matter what conclusions I came to, and I examined as many scenarios as I could, they all pointed at a fate less than desirable. I tucked the cards away and pulled my purse close to me.

When we arrived at his parents' home, I had bolstered my confidence as far as I could. All my life, my friends' parents always liked me. I was determined to win her over.

After we walked in the door, Mark introduced me around the room. Len and Jessica, already there with their kids, were friendly in their greeting. When introduced to Mark's mother, she looked me up and down, frowning, but did not speak.

The rest of the day passed without incident. On our

second day, in the afternoon, most of us were gathered in the living room conversing. I noticed that Jessica had joined us and sat next to Len. I thought this unusual since most of the time I had witnessed her busying herself with one domestic chore after another. Mark was at one end of the room play wrestling with one of his nephews. Mark's father was working outside, and not in the room. I was content listening to the conversation.

I jumped slightly when the nephew Mark was playing with let out a wild scream. The child started crying and ran directly to his grandmother, arms stretched in front of him. "Mark hurt me," he bawled grabbing at his grandmother's knees.

Mark's mother wrapped her arms protectively around her grandson and shot a glare at me that froze the room around us. "Why did you hurt him?" she snapped.

Stunned, my mouth fell open. I couldn't speak.

Len calmly looked at his mother and reached a hand over to lay on her arm. "Mom, he said that *Mark* hurt him."

Her face transformed like a cartoon vixen contemplating her latest plan, "Oh, I guess it's all in who does it."

I could see Jessica from the corner of my eye leap up and with one rapid movement make a quick exit. I looked at Mark. He remained quiet and didn't look at me. No sign of dismay anywhere near his face.

Bewilderment, anger, disgust, many strong emotions assaulted me at once. I stifled the need to lash out – it would do no good.

I mumbled a short "Excuse me" and left. I sought out the bedroom with my things in them and closed the door behind me. I tried to focus on reading the book I'd brought, but the scene in the living room kept running through my head. Over and over.

She was in the room I affirmed to myself. She saw what happened. Yet she chose to pin the blame on me. How could anyone do such a thing? As disconcerting as this was, what was more unsettling was Mark's reaction. It was Len who quietly came to my rescue. No doubt he was accustomed to defending Jessica.

I got up from my seat on the bed and grabbed for my purse. The recipes I had so painstakingly chosen with an eye toward impressing his family were not hard to find. I hadn't used them yet. Their significance slowly losing power. I buried them deep within my suitcase. I no longer saw a reason to use them. There was no need to attempt to impress anyone who was as implacable as that. My thoughts turned to Jessica. *She must love Len beyond measure*, I thought. Their relationship was strong. There were more and more cracks in mine.

Suddenly exhausted, I laid down on the bed and fell asleep.

When I emerged a couple hours later, Jessica was by herself in the laundry room, buried in freshly cleaned clothing, working the piles around her. Mark's father was still outside. The men and their matriarch hadn't moved from their spots in the living room.

Reunions

Mark had grown up in Saudia Arabia. His father worked for the largest oil company in the world and during Mark's young years he and his family were part of a contingent of Americans clustered in a community in Dhahran.

These former children who grew up together held a reunion every few years and this was one of those years. By coincidence, my own 20th high school reunion was scheduled for not too long after his.

He was traveling to Houston to attend this reunion. And he was not taking me with him. When I asked him why he didn't want me to go, he said that I wouldn't enjoy it.

Something didn't seem right about that but by this time

in our relationship, I was not sure I even wanted to go.

Earlier, I had decided I would invite him to mine even if he didn't want to take me to his. But something held me back. I hadn't even told him about it. *I should invite him*, I thought. But I put off telling him about it.

As the time got closer though I became more and more concerned that he wasn't planning on taking me to his reunion. His excitement was high. And I was apprehensive. I reminded myself that we had been together many years now and it was okay to do things separately. Important even, to retain separate interests. Still, the feeling that something wasn't quite right stayed with me, getting stronger and stronger.

I enjoyed myself the week he was away – spending time alone was a balm that helped renew my spirit.

Soon after his return, he invited me over to look at his pictures. He'd had a great time, he said, and wanted to show me the multitude of photos he took. A chance to relive the joy of his visit.

We sat down on his couch and started going through the photos. As he talked about the many things he did, I began to see a theme in his pictures. He was with the same two women in every one of them. He shrugged it off and said they were simply old friends.

"Are you sure they are just friends?" I said with mixed emotions.

"Yes," he said, returning to his reminiscences.

"They are in every picture," I said losing the battle of my growing jealousy. "They look like more than friends."

"No," he said with obvious irritation. "Absolutely not."

My intuition switched from *something is not right* to *this is why he didn't want me around.*

I pondered on this for several days. I had to trust him. Trust is a central issue to a solid relationship. And I did trust him to tell me the truth. Then I hit on what was really bothering me.

We were a couple. A partnership. It was the partnership part that was missing. He wanted me around when it was convenient. But when it wasn't, as in when he wanted female attention apart from me, it wasn't in his thoughts. I was expendable. He could "forget" me until I became necessary again. Until the other two people's attention went away. That's not how I pictured romantic partnerships. I wanted someone whose first thoughts went to me instead of other women, friends or not.

My feelings were changing. Cracks in the wall of our foundation were starting to grow into craters. I no longer wanted him to come with me to my reunion. But I thought it a betrayal if I went alone. In the end, I chose instead not to attend.

Pushing Too Far

Mark was going on vacation and he asked me to come along. We'd spent time together on day trips to the mountains to hike or take in the scenery. Now he wanted me to spend seven days with him in the backcountry of Colorado. I hoped this trip would revitalize our bond.

But even being in nature together could not save our relationship from deteriorating. This camping trip would be a turning point test. We drove mostly two-lane highways with no real agenda, stopping at various viewpoints, deciding where we would go as we went. Or, I should say, he decided where we should go.

About mid-way through our trip, we were driving without having stopped for a while when I began to get the feeling I needed eat. By this time in my life, I had learned that one trigger for a migraine attack was not eating when my body told me that I needed nourishment.

I told Mark we had to stop to eat, explaining my reason. He didn't want to stop. He had a destination he was shooting for and decided we would keep going until we hit that stopping point. Normally, I wouldn't protest much. The give in give-and-take. But that day I knew it would not be good for either of us if we kept going. I told him we had to stop and launched into an extended explanation of why in case it passed him by the first time.

He returned my explanation with a firm "You can hold out a little longer." I knew that wasn't going to happen.

"Look," I said pointing at an upcoming billboard, "There is a restaurant in the next town. Let's stop there. I can't go much longer."

"I don't want to stop there," he said, crinkling up his nose. "It doesn't look good,"

Without looking my direction, he continued driving through the town and right past the restaurant.

I began to sense the symptoms start that always preceded a migraine for me. I knew them well. But there were no more options for sustenance along our route.

By the time he found his destination, our campsite for the night, I had one-sided head pain growing stronger. The process had begun, and I had no way to stop it now. Included in that was the queasiness that was more and more accompanying the migraine episodes. After putting up the tent, I had reached the end of my ability to function. I had to lie down.

"Come on," he said nonchalantly, "Let's go get something to eat."

"I can't," I said, crawling gently into the tent. "I have to lie down." I knew my upset stomach would only throw any food right back up. At this point, I had to ride it out.

"Come on," anger flexing in his voice. "You said you had to eat, so let's go get something to eat."

"I'm beyond that now," I said hoping he would just go away. It was painful to talk.

"So, you're not coming?" I could see his jaw flexing in

front of the waning sunlight of day. Sunlight that shot painful arrows through my head.

"No, you go ahead." I said, hoping to avoid an argument.

"I'll go by myself then," he said in staccato jabs before stomping off.

"Okay, you do that," I said whispering to myself.

I lay on the hard ground praying silently but fervently that I would not have to vomit. Taking long, slow, deep breaths in hopes I could quell the upset's power. We were a long walk from the public restrooms.

He returned an hour later. I don't know what he did the rest of that evening as I fell asleep immediately upon his return and stayed asleep until morning.

When I awoke to the sunshine streaming through our tent opening, I smiled to myself. The light didn't darken my head pain anymore. The migraine was mostly gone. A former shadow of itself, not the enemy it was the day before.

We picked up our things before going to breakfast. The restaurant at the campsite wasn't too far off, but we drove to it anyway.

Things seemed a little tense between us. He was quiet but amicable. We were almost done eating breakfast when I said, "I want to go back to the campground restrooms and brush my teeth."

I had gone into the restaurant restroom before we ate and realized it was not as clean as the one we just left. In fact, it was caked in filth. And the cleaner restrooms were a short quarter of a mile behind us.

Anger shot across his face, flaring his nostrils. "There is no reason to go back," he said looking at me with steely eyes before announcing, "We are leaving from here."

"I don't want to brush my teeth here," I said crinkling my forehead, "It's not clean. It won't take very long to go back."

"We're not going back," he shot back at me. "you should've brushed your teeth before we left."

"So, really" I said, "You're not going to let me go back?"

"Go brush your teeth here." It was a command, not a request.

"No," I said, "I'll wait. Thank you." The anger was building in me. He could choose to keep me from our former campsite, but he was not going to tell me where I was going to brush my teeth.

"Go brush your teeth," he enunciated each word.

"No, I'll wait."

"Go brush your teeth NOW."

The last word in his sentence sent a chill down my back. My first thought was, *I'm here in backcountry Colorado with no way home except with him.* I looked into his eyes and I didn't like what I saw. I could let my pride continue a losing battle. Or I could de-escalate the situation now by capitulating.

I grabbed my toothbrush out of my purse. Carrying both to the restroom, I got up and disappeared behind the door. Standing within the walls of the Ladies' Room, I stuffed the toothbrush back in my purse. "I'm not brushing my teeth here," I said out loud without even looking to see if I had company.

Dirty as it was, the walls of the restroom were more comforting than the table I just left. I knew he wouldn't come in after me no matter how long I stayed. My mind started churning the moment around. I had to get calm and I had to build up the strength to get through the rest of the day. His manner had a jarring effect on me. Frightening. I stayed in the Ladies Room long enough to get my courage up to go face him.

When I left probably 15 minutes later, I walked directly outside. There was a small farmer's market in the parking lot, and I welcomed the opportunity to delay getting in the car with him. I walked around aimlessly, eyeing the vegetables, forcing a smile at the vendors. After some minutes I could feel him shadowing me.

"We need to go," he said quieter but in a still firm, slightly irritated tone of voice.

I didn't say anything but followed him to his vehicle. We drove in silence the next two hours. I welcomed the solitude. I needed to think. To mull over this ugly side of him. To consider what our relationship really was, what I was willing to put up with to allow it to continue, and whether it was all worth it. Watching the passing scenery was comforting and allowed my mind to back off from the hurt I felt. Lingering to process the nuances.

Thinking over the past few days, thinking over the past few years, my mind stirred with the incidents that were significant. The times where he made all the decisions, without input from me. The times he refused to listen to my needs. It suddenly hit me. I was nothing more than an object to complement his time, like the tent that served its purpose when we went camping. Something to complete his idea of what his experience should be like. Not my own philosophy -- spending time with someone who you long to share experience within a give-and-take romance. It was quite the opposite; all about what Mark wanted.

Lost in my thoughts I suddenly felt his hand on mine. "I'm sorry," he said looking at me. The apology given quietly, no further command in his voice.

"MMMM hmmm," I said looking down at his hand on mine, then back into his eyes. I studied those eyes. They gave me no clear answers. "Okay."

He seemed remorseful, but I couldn't find the motivation. Was it because he regretted his actions and had silently vowed to learn from the encounter? Or because he wanted his compliant travel partner back? The companion who provides the "yes" to every whim he wants to indulge. Or something in between? Knowing the answer to this would certainly enlighten the quandary I was in. If I had to admit it to myself, I knew the answer. I was fast losing my resistance to fighting the truth. I had begun to realize that the longer I stayed with him the more this angry and controlling part of him showed itself. I knew that relationships were work. But this one was beginning to feel one-sided.

Alter Egos

I was an audacious, strong-willed child with larger-than-life ambitions. At the age of 3 or 4, I demanded to be able to ride my tricycle to my grandparents' house. We lived on an Illinois farm that was half a mile down the rocky country road from my grandparents' farm.

My mother, worn to frustration with my repeated requests, finally gave in. I pedaled down our lane to the gravel road with great confidence and verve. My energy high, my spirits soaring, I was on top of the world.

My parents were not so confident. They drove at a snail's pace about 20 feet behind me the entire way. I was sure they were an inch from stopping me and swooping my trike up into the back of the old pick-up truck. I kept my eyes looking forward and didn't look back. To my glee, I made it to my grandparents' doorstep with no parental interference.

Two or three years later, I recall a different experience. A family gathering at my grandparents' farm. Several relations standing in an open area next to the pasture holding a couple of horses. An older girl cousin asked to ride one of the horses.

Someone took the horse out of the field and brought it into the interior of our gathering. I listened as my grandfather warned the group that no one should ride the horse – it hadn't been ridden in some time. Looking at the horse, it's eyes frightened, its jerky movements displaying a sense of nervousness, I hoped that common sense would take over and no one would get on it.

My cousin was preparing to get on the horse. "No," I wanted to scream at her, the dread building in my mind. I opened my mouth to voice my concern. Just then, someone grabbed me under the arms and lifted me upward. Flailing about, I tried to put my feet on the horse's hindquarters and push away. "No, I don't want to go on the horse," I screamed.

It was all to no avail. I found myself clutching to my cousin's sides, my legs straddling the horse. But not for long.

The extra weight must have been too much for the skittish animal. It roared up on its hind legs spilling me off the back. My uncle, closest to the fray, reached out and grabbed me before I hit the ground.

Still facing the horse, I saw it take off with my cousin grasping its mane in a death crouch. Both my cousin and the horse soared past the house and disappeared into the orchard.

I was terrified watching my cousin. In the waning minutes, my legs wobbled, and my insides churned. I knew my cousin was in great peril. As I looked around, the adults appeared to have little concern.

As if by command, after what seemed like a lifetime, the horse and its rider appeared trotting back to the group.

The horse was put back in the pasture. The group of relatives ambled back to the farmhouse, not one in distress but me. Not even my older cousin.

Somewhere in the intervening years, something changed in me. Two sides. The person who never wants to be seen or cause trouble or venture too far into the fearful unknown. Vs. the fearless goddess. Driven and motivated. Alter egos wrestling for acceptability. Striving to win. One holding the other back, the other striving for the comfort of control and placidity.

Back to School Again

Two years post undergraduate degree, I was frustrated.

My career stalemated; I hadn't found a job. Still working as an admin, I wanted a job with more upward mobility. And one I could feel good about doing. I didn't feel challenged in the type of work I'd done since high school. I thought if I was going to be a career woman, then I had to find something more suitable to a career path. Something I could be proud of.

Mark had worked as a computer programmer and was doing well. He suggested I consider programming as an occupation saying that there were jobs in abundance for that line of work. I decided to consider it.

I found a post-graduate program at a private university that was one year in length. The program was intense and had a good reputation. Once again, I found myself in school.

The Last Straw

We were supposed to meet at one of Mark's favorite restaurants. It was a Friday night ritual we had. As always, I got there a little early and instead of going in to wait for him as was the custom, I decided to sit in my car. I had come from a stressful day at work and I needed a little alone time. If I went inside to wait for him, there would be other people around. This night I just needed to decompress.

I drove through the rows of cars looking for his to make sure he hadn't gotten there early. I knew he didn't like to wait for me. No sign of him.

I sat in my car doing some deep breathing exercises, a favored remedy to stress. Looking around, he was not anywhere in sight. I watched every car entering the parking lot.

I did a short meditation. Still no sign of him. I was starting to feel "back to normal" so I picked up my book to read. An encouraging volume urging readers to take a stand in their relationships. Express their needs. Especially women who tended to give more than take. I knew I fit in this category and I was trying to find an alternative to breaking up. In the months since our dismal vacation, I'd tried to convince myself that all couples go through difficult times. Breaking up was not the answer. I didn't want that failure on my record, my past with men as discouraging as it was.

After a few minutes, I could sense a tugging at my conscience. I decided I better go inside and wait for Mark despite the comfort I was getting from my alone time in the car. This restaurant had a rather roomy waiting area with chairs placed just outside their dining area. I tucked the book back in my bag and headed for the door.

The minute I walked in the door, I saw Mark. He jumped to his feet, red-faced. "Where have you been?" he bellowed so loudly that people from across the room turned to look.

"I was in my car waiting for you," I said as low-keyed and controlled as I could muster.

"You've been outside all this time?"

"All what time? How long have you been here?"

"Long enough," he growled. I looked around at the people staring at us. He seemed completely unaware and continued yelling at me for being late and keeping him waiting.

I stood there staring at him. He always kept me waiting and I never responded like this. This rage was becoming an everyday scenario. The tenderness and warmth that he showed me in the first few years of our being together had slowly morphed into what I was watching now. In silence I took it in. Failure or not, I couldn't stay in this relationship.

After a few elongated minutes passed, he seemed to wear himself out. He looked at me with disgust and growled, "Well, I guess we better go in."

I stood there for a minute thinking. *Go on,* I told myself, *this is your chance. The opportunity you've been waiting for. Leave now. End this.* I turned and left without a word.

<u>Breaking Up</u>

When I got home that evening, I started to feel guilty about walking out on him. Me, who never made waves, had angered an already angry man. I was sure of it. And my go-to response was to apologize. I wanted to be strong and not give in to the guilt that was baring down on me, but it got the better of me. So, when I knew he would be home later in the evening, I called him.

He didn't answer my call. I waited and called again 20 minutes later. Still, he didn't answer. It was a relief to me, and I didn't leave a message. I needed more time to think this through. I was glad that I at least could identify that it was guilt driving my need to contact him, not that I really felt I had done something so catastrophic that it deserved the tongue-lashing I got.

He was going on a solo camping trip the next day, so he would be out of reach for a week. That would allow me enough time to decide if I really wanted to break up or if I would let slide yet another incident that I found demeaning.

I reveled in the next few days. I felt free and more confident than I had felt for years. On Wednesday, I came home to a blinking light on my answering machine. It was Mark. He wanted to talk to me and said he would call in the evening.

I'd spent those days weighing my options. I could stay in a loveless relationship because it meant I had one. Or I could risk going out there again. That meant I could find what I really wanted. Or I could never find it.

By this time, I had gone through so many failures with men that I started to fret that a lasting relationship would never happen for me. The thought entered my mind but drew less power than ever before. I marveled that I didn't feel as devastated by this prognosis as I had decades before.

I was in my late thirties and had spent seven years in a

relationship that was dead-end. It wasn't all I had built it up to be. I'd outgrown the prom dream. And I had survived. Even adjusted to it, finding peace and happiness despite its loss.

Having acknowledged that to myself, I determined to go through with the break-up. I just didn't want to do it while he was still on his vacation. When the phone range later in the evening, I stifled my impulse to answer it. I could wait another couple of days to regain my freedom.

He called when he got home from his trip. His demeanor so different from our last encounter, he immediately began telling me the highlights of his trip. Like nothing had happened. When there was a break in his flow of conversation, I told him I was glad he called. I wanted to talk to him.

"I know what you're going to say," he said, tensely with a hint of resignation. "You're breaking up with me."

"Yes," I said. "It's just not working."

"I knew you would, just like before." He reminded me of the story of his broken engagement earlier in his life. I knew the story. He and the woman had had a big blow-up argument, much like the one we had. He knew losing his temper caused her to end their engagement and had apologized to her. She responded by telling him she was becoming a nun. He still grappled with why. Now I was leaving him devastated too.

"It's more than the argument at the restaurant," I said, "It's been coming for a long time."

Two years, I recalled to myself. It had taken me two years to do this. Two too long.

"Hmmm. I'd like to remain friends." He was calm, no rage like I'd seen at the restaurant. An unnerving calm, but calm nonetheless. It was trying to speak to me, but I ignored it.

Instead, I felt a surge, almost a physical uplift. I'd done it, and he was accepting my choice without debate. I'd spoken out for what I wanted, instead of giving in to the overpowering command telling me I had no right to. I was shaken and energetic at the same time.

Chapter 8 - No More Luna Moths

<u>Limerance</u>

Years earlier, I had ventured into probably my favorite bookstore of all time. It was a welcoming three-story structure with endless shelves of my favorite pastime. I had an itch in my soul I needed to scratch. A personal truth expedition. This urge attacked me at various times in my life and I had learned to drop everything and follow its whim. On this day, it was strong though I had no sense as to which direction to go, or even where to begin.

I found myself ambling without direction in a corner upstairs. Fingering the spines of book after book, I was beginning to think I had been misled by a wayward notion. Until my fingers landed on a nondescript brick-red binding with white letters. *Love and Limerance*, it said. I pulled the book out with interest. *Love and Limerance, The Experience of Being in Love*, by Dorothy Tennov.

The internal prickling dissolved. This was it. I was sure – the fulfillment of my quest for the day. I flipped the book over and started reading the back. It talked of thriving, and, at the same time, dying on the edge of your feelings for a love interest, a deep recessed need for reciprocity from that spotlight person, and a compulsive desire for that someone intensified by adversity. Most important, it talked about the craving for one's true love – the belief that there is only one passionate resolution to your heart's desire.

I flipped through the hallowed pages. It described unrequited love as an emotional tornado. Story after story of people who, like me, seemed to fall into love hard, fast and heavy. Some without any provocation. The phenomenon divergent in character, feel and perspective than the typical act of falling in love. I knew this all too well as I had experienced both. Having just come from the normal kind in Mark, it contrasted so profusely from the all-consuming fire I'd felt for my high school crush. And very nearly Dante. The stark difference leading me to wonder what inside of me made me *long* (the book's oh-so-appropriate word for it) so strongly for an impossible situation. Why were my emotions so powerful, when there were so many people who never experienced this concern at all?

I grasped the book like the last buoy on an endless ocean. This was a part of the solution to my puzzle. It had to be. If nothing more than reassurance that I was not singularly experiencing the phenomenon. The comfort of knowing I am not in the choppy sea by myself.

Over the years since, I'd pondered the limerant phenomenon. This occurrence had to be another biochemical aberrance. Somehow attached to the attraction biochemicals that were so natural in everyone. But could find no evidence in the science. No one had yet explained this thing that affected this smaller portion of humans. Disappointed, I wasn't ready to give it up yet.

Caffeine

One of the prescriptions I had tried early in my migraine history worked like a miracle. If I could catch a migraine in its early stages and take this pill, the migraine would almost immediately begin to recede. The relief was incredible. Like one of those films of a storm quickly receding when shown in reverse. All the more puzzling to me was the fact that this drug was made up of the simple ingredient caffeine.

I had to deal with a few annoying side effects. The feeling that every nerve in my body carried its own lightning charge striking each nerve ending with an energy-draining zap. But this sensation was well worth enduring to end the siege of pain and disability that came with an attack.

After a few short years on this drug, the doctors pulled it from me. There were other drugs, they said, that worked better. But after trying these other drugs, I found they had no effect on me. I might as well have taken a sugar pill for all the good they did. We would have to keep trying they said, as taking caffeine was not a good solution. They gave no reason for their sudden reversal.

It wasn't too hard to figure out that I could get caffeine in other ways. Not a coffee drinker, I turned to tea. Black tea in its typical form was sufficient to ward off a migraine. Cola drinks worked well in a pinch.

I was only mildly concerned that I was going against medical advice. But it was worth it to me. From past doctors' complacence, I had started to take less stock in their advice. And I was tired of losing chunks of my life to a migraine attack. I determined to beat that life-stealing thief at its own game.

Slipping Backward

Mark continued to call me with the same intensity as if we were still together. We still got together as friends. So much so that it began to feel like we had never parted.

One of the things we enjoyed doing together was going to garage sales. And this turned into a weekly event for us. He liked finding bargains and the area I lived in was populated with more well-to-do families whose garage sales reeked of bargains.

On one day we happened onto a garage sale that had four white plastic lawn chairs for sale. The four were being sold as a set. I asked Mark if he was interested in them. His answer a pronounced "no." Two were in really good shape, the second two were not in such good shape. I had a small patio, so I offered the women selling the chairs a small price for the two best ones. It was less than the whole amount but larger than half the total. They agreed to my offer.

I was loading the two I'd bought into the car when Mark came up behind me carrying the second set of two.

"I thought you didn't want the chairs," I said to him as he loaded them into the back of the car.

"I changed my mind," he said.

"Okay," An ominous chord hit my senses. Set my nerves to vibrate. I tried to push it back.

When we got back to my home, I took my small purchases inside. When I returned, he had unloaded the two more damaged chairs and was getting ready to leave.

"Hey, wait a minute," I said. "Those are your chairs. The ones in your car are mine."

"No," he said, "Those are mine. These are yours."

"What is going on? I bought the best two," I said. "Those are the ones in the car."

"No, you're wrong," he was starting to get angry. "Those are mine."

The ominous chord returned with the sense that he was doing this on purpose. "So, you're not going to give me my chairs?"

"No," he glared at me.

"Okay," I said, trying to keep my cool. I didn't want to continue arguing over the chairs, and I knew he would not give in. "Take them all. I don't want the bad chairs," I said.

He loaded up all the chairs and left.

I was still seething. The chairs were inconsequential. Immaterial. What was important was that it was a reminder of why I had called it quits between us. His materialism, his choice to put physical objects ahead of me was one of my top reasons. In this case, the physical objects were a couple of $.50 chairs. I knew he knew what he was doing with the chairs. But it was more important for him to walk away with the chairs than give me any consideration. He might even be doing it to punish me for our breakup. I thought about how much time we were spending together. I wanted to be friends. But I felt he had abused his privilege to my friendship. Most importantly, I was not going to let someone, anyone, walk all over me like that.

Not anymore. There was a time when I would. But a new me was emerging. Decision set my jaw to rigid. It was the time to make it clear that we were broken up, whether it cost me a friendship or not.

<u>Mama's Opinion</u>

In the weeks that followed, I'd turned down his requests to get together, reminding him that we had broken up. I continued to talk to him on the phone and we were in the middle of a pleasant conversation one day when the mood changed quickly.

He fell silent for a few moments before saying, "I talked to my mother and she thinks you led me to the alter and left me standing there."

"What?" I said a little bewildered. "Where did that come from?"

He repeated what he had just said and added, "And *I* think you did too."

I had to think for a moment. Too many different emotions went bouncing through my head. Most of them rising from the shock of what I'd just heard. Deciding to treat his accusation as logically as I could, I said, "At what point in the last seven years did we become engaged?"

"That's not the point . . ."

"It certainly is," I said, allowing my emotions some escape, "You can only leave a person at the alter if you have some sort of understanding that you are planning to get married. There was only one time we even talked about it. Some five years ago now. And as I recall, you weren't very excited about the idea then. You've said nothing about it since."

"I thought we were going to get married," he said.

"When did you think you were going to let me know? On the day you arbitrarily decided would be our wedding day?" My voice was getting louder the angrier I got.

He fell silent. There was a long pause. I tried to regain my calm. I felt a nudge push upward from my solar plexus. Its strength pushing at my weakness.

"I think it's best if we don't talk anymore." I said after gathering my courage.

"Fine with me." The connection on the phone ended abruptly. He hand hung up on me.

I had to take some deep breaths after replacing the receiver in its cradle. Over the time I'd known his mother, she had surprised me more than once with her beliefs and judgments. Every time, it had thrown me off guard. Mark, when it came to the subject of his mother's view, I couldn't read so well. But this really stopped me in my tracks. I couldn't comprehend that he honestly believed what he was telling me. Was it Mama's prompting or could he really believe this? And if so, what kind of impudence did it take to float such a ridiculous notion?

I flashed back over the years. I could not find one clue that he was thinking marriage. I certainly abandoned that idea years earlier.

As I pondered this, I began to realize that his indignation at my choice to end our romance was showing. His bitterness building from the chair incident to this, with Mama fueling the fire.

Time Off

It really was over now. The finality was an emotion all its own, eerie but strong, with components of loss and emptiness. I would need a mourning period to get back on my feet. But within myself I saw this as a hurtle that would lead to something better. And I was confident I would get past it.

I decided that I would give myself a period of solitude. Healing time. After that, I wasn't quite sure. I had outgrown the church singles' group and left it behind after I started dating Mark. I had no desire to go back. It had served its purpose in my life. I wanted new horizons.

After a buffer period of glorious alone time, I would be ready to go out again. Not to start looking for Mr. Right. Curiously, I had no burning desire to jump right into my next relationship. I just wanted to make some new friends. But for now, being by myself for long periods of healing was a comfortable place to be. I relished the quiet and calm. I meditated and read. I wrote down my thoughts and feelings. Starting a gratitude journal, I gained a new awareness of the good in my life.

Trying Poison

I entered the office of my normally stoic migraine doctor. The tips of his cheeks had a flushed look. An epic smile pointed toward his brilliant eyes. He had asked me to make an appointment. A specialist in headache management, I was one of his problem patients.

"There's something new on the horizon," he said gesturing to the chair in front of his desk.

I sat down to listen.

"Sometimes medicine comes into solutions by accident," he started. "Have you ever heard of Botox injections?"

"Maybe," I said with dampening enthusiasm. It seemed to stick in my mind from some obscure source I couldn't recall. "Isn't that related to botulism?"

"Botox," he continued oblivious to my reticence, "is made from bacteria that causes botulism. It has been used successfully by cosmetic doctors to minimize fine lines and wrinkles." He paused before going on. "There is a doctor who found that several of his Botox patients were helped in another area of their lives by these injections. They reported having fewer migraines."

"So, you want to try that with me?" I asked cautiously.

"Yes," he said, "It seems extreme, but I think it's worth a try. The procedure is simple. Two shots into the forehead."

"Okay," I said in slow motion. My mind was racing through the outcomes. On one end of the spectrum, I could be on the cutting edge of a miracle break-through. No more migraines. Or even if it created diminished migraines. What a hope that was. But at what cost? I would be intentionally allowing someone to put a needle containing poison in my head. Was I that desperate? The answer came quickly. Yes. Yes, I was.

"Let's do it," I said.

<u>Passivity and the Luna Moth</u>

I once found a greeting card that I've kept for a long time. It spoke to me with such fervor. On the front is a comical little moth floating through the air with the words "The male Luna moth, through his highly developed sense of smell, can detect a female five miles away." You open up the card and it says, "But does he call? Noooooooo!!" I'd run into so many men in my lifetime who exhibited this same type of come-hither-but-stop-just-short-of-actually-doing-anything-about-it behavior, I was beginning to think that men no longer believed in asking a woman out. Mark had been one of the rare exceptions in my life to this point. But I'd come to the end of that chapter in my life.

As I was adjusting to life without Mark my mind began wandering to a man I knew through my work.

Leo was a client of the attorney I worked for. He was

tall and handsome, and very personable. Always kind and patient. Leo would call for my boss and spend the first 15 minutes talking to me. The subjects he covered ran the gamut between superficial – did I know there was a famous cartoon character whose neighbor bore his last name? – to more intimidate – his recent experience of overcoming cancer in a very personal and private area of his body.

Up to this point, I'd felt our conversations were simply friendly. That friendly feeling shifted when one day's conversation started with him talking about his brother's successful business. After several minutes of boasting its virtues, he revealed to me where the business was located. This revelation the crescendo of his speech. He paused. A classic pregnant pause. A flash in my mind of his face, eyes searching, cheeks still, head tilted in a pose of expectation. I responded to that perceived expectation with authentic enthusiasm, "That's my old hometown. It's where I grew up." My voice lifted to the joy of discovering commonality. His response, a flat and even, "Is that so?"

After that conversation ended and I had returned to work, the full impact of that expectation component hit me. I had never told him anything about my hometown. Yet, from how the interaction arose, it struck me that he knew this before I told him. This premise captivated me. And signaled to me a shift on his part from friendly banter to romantic interest. In hindsight, it should've sent my creepy meter into awareness mode.

I found myself thinking about him more and more. But I was puzzled. He didn't come across to me like a Luna moth kind of guy. He was a take charge go-getter whose successes, I was sure, came from his willingness to take risks. Still, his behavior toward me seemed curious. And oftentimes, flirtatious. It was all the trappings of being hit on without the final step.

I had to know where I stood. Too often, I had left

Mere Sense

feelings hanging in the air. The memory of Dante's music video still clinging tightly to my memories left an uncomfortable and silent yearning. Crying out for an end to unresolved, unfinished business.

My instincts told me I would be rejected. I knew I would probably make myself look foolish, but the alternative was no longer acceptable. The mind craves conclusion. I had to know whether what I was seeing was real interest or just flirtatious. Or worse, an artful way to feed his ego.

It wasn't long after making the decision to find out, he called into the office. The timing was great. There were few prying ears as the office was nearly empty that day. I took a deep breath and asked if I could ask him something personal. "Yes," he said cautiously. I asked if there was anything going on between us. He was surprised. No, shocked was more the reaction. He explained that he lived with his girlfriend and would never consider pursuing anything outside that relationship. I felt the red heat up my cheeks, but I thanked him, as graciously as I could muster, for clearing up the confusion. I wished him well and hung up with a catch in my throat.

My embarrassment encircled and consumed me. Eating deep within me and my sensitivities. I wanted to run away and hide. I knew I had to pull from within me more courage than I currently had within me so I could face him again. A requirement of my job. I chastised my inability to read the situation correctly. How I must have embarrassed him, made him feel uncomfortable. Placing him in an awkward position did more to suffer my mood than my own embarrassment.

Goodbye Luna Moth

Throughout the day I tried my best to find where I had gone so wrong. He had talked about his divorce, but never about his girlfriend. If I'd known that he had one, I certainly would not have asked him what I did. I didn't want to break up anyone's relationship. But we'd had so many conversations that I thought sure he would've at least brought her up once. Sadness, embarrassment, and anger made alternate appearances through my heart. I went home that afternoon as mystified as I started the day, not having been able to pinpoint where I could've misread the signals so completely.

Nerves took over the next few days. I hoped I would not have to talk to him. And I didn't. Odd that he didn't call, considering the deal he was working on at the time. I was sure that I had completely thrown him off, probably insulted him. And I felt ashamed for having done so. But as the days passed, I also began to feel relief too.

If I could never read the true meaning in his intentions toward me, how could any sort of relationship work? *Communication, including those silly nonverbal signals people put out, is so important to a relationship,* I thought. As I contemplated this, I smiled for the first time at the situation. A smile with a melancholy blue around it.

Fledgling to my mind, a thought surfaced. *Everything will be alright. Everything always turns out the way it should in the end.* A lightness, airy and warm, like hot chocolate on a cold day, spread through me. These words not new to me. It was an axiom I had used for years when I needed to boost my spirits. Different this time, the words traveled over my nerves shearing off their jagged edges, releasing their tautness. Their truth a feeling, no longer single words to comprehend but one action. Like breathing.

Good was happening. I had gotten an offer from one of the companies I'd applied to for a computer programming job. I gave my two-week notice ready to head off into the tech world and leave the administrative assistant world behind. This event seemed choreographed to my intent to move on.

Over the following two weeks, I still did not talk to Leo. Four-thirty on my last day on the job, my relief reached its

Mere Sense

summit. Half an hour and I could walk out the door, confident I would never speak to Leo again. Then, the phone rang.

No, it can't be. What are the odds? There was no way to tell who it was on the other end of the phone, but my stomach took a synchronistic dive anyway. I cheerily picked up the phone with my professional greeting.

"Hello Monica." The sound of his voice punching my relief in the stomach.

"Oh, hi Leo." I pulled every micron of enthusiasm from my deflated relief into the sentence as I could find. "He's in his office. I'll ring him."

"No, I want to talk to you."

Silence. "Oh . . . kay. What . . . can . . . I . . . do for you?" The words stumbled out of my mouth as I silently prayed, *Please let it be a fax or document, or some other last minute task.*

"I hear you're leaving."

"Yeah," I said.

Immediately words sprayed from my mouth. My intended career change. The business degree that did not yield any possibilities. Going into graduate school in computer programming. Staying in administrative work until I found an entry position, which wasn't easy given my age.

Not normally a nervous talker, I didn't know where those words were coming from. *Stop!* I yelled at myself. When I finally lassoed my tongue and there was silence, I sat holding my breath.

"I wish you the best," he said, "Are you going to write to me?"

Confused curiosity replaced my former uncomfortableness.

"I'm sorry," I said trying not to sound too dumfounded. "What did you say?"

"We're friends, right? Are you going to write to me?"

Silence. The voice in my head stilled to counting the

seconds. 1001. 1002. 1003.

"Ahh, yeah, sure, okay. If you want me to," I finally said.

"Yes," he said. Then he ended our conversation.

Realization was swift. It was the worst of the three scenarios I had surmised two weeks before. His attitude toward me not real interest. I was a tool for admiration. Someone to boost the ego. Nothing more. Less than human.

As I promised, I wrote to him – once, carefully keeping my correspondence superficial, knowing full well that I would not receive a response. When I did not, I considered myself released from my obligation.

Bye-bye, Luna moth.

Ammonia

The smell hit my child's nostrils in one powerful punch. Sending its evil messenger straight into the muscles that surrounded my skull. Simultaneously, making my stomach arch forward in a heave-like motion.

"Yuck," catapulted from my mouth with little precursory thought. The whine of odiferous poison from the bucket of ammonia-filled water my mother thrust into my hands permeated me to the core.

My mother retracted the bucket slightly from my personal space, only to return it a split second later. Her face took on a don't-give-me-any-excuses sternness. I knew from the look on her face that I had no choice. She was not going to listen to my explanation that the toxic liquid made me feel sick. It had no apparent effect on her.

"I know you don't like cleaning," she said bringing her best disciplinarian fierceness forward, "But I want you to clean the bathroom."

"But it stinks." I protested, despite knowing any attempt was useless. I tried to push the evil venom away from me.

"Take this," she commanded, "Now."

She turned and disappeared down the hallway. I put my fingers around the bucket handle, turned, and sloshed toward the bathroom. Trying to hold it as far from my nose as possible.

My 9-year-old's logic searched frantically for an escape. The solution it came up with was to breathe through my mouth and work as fast as I could. I stuck my hands into the ammonia-tinged water, grabbed the rag, and started scrubbing as hard and as fast as I could.

Within moments, I began to feel my fingers and hands revolting. I dropped the rag, still mouth-breathing, and looked down on them. They were red. Angry red. My attention switched to my mouth. As incredible as the assault on my hands and nose and head and stomach was, my mouth seemed to take the brunt of it. Dry as a desert, the awful smell seemed to morph into a physical sensation in my mouth, seeping into the droughted crevices.

This was more than I could ignore. I dropped the rag into the bucket and reached for a towel. Pressing my tongue against it, I tried to wipe away the irritation. When that didn't work, I stuffed the towel further into my mouth. Twisting the mouthful of towel around in circles, all I accomplished was to make my mouth drier.

In a fit of fury that bordered on panic, I pulled the towel from my mouth and threw it on the floor. Then I scrubbed and wiped and cleaned and hit every surface I could find with the rag. When I could stand it no longer, I ran for my room.

Yelling "I'm done", I pulled the door of my bedroom shut and threw myself on the bed.

Caustic Relationships

Ammonia in its place as a cleaning agent has its purpose, and it fulfills it like no other substance can. But it can also be caustic, meaning that it is corrosive. It can wipe out other substances that come across its path. In small doses, most people can tolerate it. To others, very little of it leads to destruction. I am in the latter group.

I was beginning to see how certain people were like ammonia to me. The Swan Killer. The Luna Moth. To most people, their corrosive powers had little effect. But to me, their caustic nature corroded away at my wellbeing.

My nature was to always see the best in people. Which meant that sometimes I was deceived. Like with Leo, the Luna Moth. At other times, I would meet someone immediately and know I needed to be cautious. Like Lorelei, the Swan Killer. The difference now was that I was beginning to trust that judgement and not question it like I always had. And also to find the courage to release those people from my life.

Writing Code

I was happy. All the long, hard years going to school and working, both full-time, was about to pay off. I had a job as a computer programmer. I could leave administrative work behind and be the professional I had worked so hard to become.

Writing code seemed right. In programming you set down pre-determined phrases in the correct pattern to make the program do what you want it to do. If you don't do them in the correct order, if your logic doesn't make sense to the machine, your program stalls or loops or crashes. It's all a matter of deciding your destination and finding the right way to get there.

I had gone through a long-term relationship that was unsuitable for both of us. It had ended, and I was still going strong. I survived. Now, I was a career woman. In charge of my own future. A little older. A little wiser. It didn't fit the original plan, but I finally had an accomplishment I could be proud of.

My problem all this time, I was sure, was that I hadn't been using the right logic diagram for my life.

Building a Collage with Decorations from the Past

In the enclosure that is our life, pictures decorate the walls. These pictures are the memories of what has come before. Varying in their size, shape, and brilliance. Some are so vague and distant that we can't make out an outline. They are the fluff whose sole purpose is to move us from one significant event to another.

But the memories of significance, the sharp, vivid images whose color is so dazzling you can't look at them too long are the ones that hold the most meaning. They show us who we are and why we exist. They are the shapers – the evolvers – that thrust us often without clear direction toward personal cultivation. They form us with, but more often without, our cooperation into who we are meant to be.

Though we most often put our efforts into trying to forget them, those brightly colored pictures demand our attention. They carry pain or shame or the loss of innocence to our own idea of the goal of happiness. But we can only come to true happiness when we confront them. Ask them to share their underlying message.

Asking is our first step. Asking opens the door to what lies beneath. A craving in the soul. It's no longer an option – you must build these memories into a collage of understanding. The drive being stronger than any notion that belies any biological urge.

This process is insidiously slow, with devious truths and false turns. Sometimes it becomes necessary to dig at the memory again and again until you can loosen it enough to pluck it from its place in randomness before adding it to your collage of meaning.

This digging can frustrate as most often your surface

desire is to bury those memories obscurely to avoid the hurt it causes. But your deeper desire always wins. And you dig and burrow as if tunneling with the tiniest of spoons.

The reward can only come when you finally extract it from its randomness and put it squarely in its true spot on the collage. Only then can you experience your salvation. Only then can you truly be released from the gnawing of its influence and let it shine and warm you with new significance.

The collage spreads the sunlight of deeper meaning that glows in accordance with other memories of its kind and your *Aha* moment releases your tumult's original hold on you. Freedom and forgiveness are the ultimate glory. The ultimate release to true joy.

I was still moving toward this goal. Stuck desperately in the grip of memories that would not yet release me. Holding me in a deep pit of my own making, with the shreds of confusion still pushing me toward the light.

Chapter 9 - The Gifted Child Becomes the Highly Sensitive Person

<u>Meeting My Third Angel</u>

Unease gnawed at my thoughts. It had been a day where my focus flitted about, going its own way only to stop mid-flight and choose a different path. I was glad to be on my way home from an unproductive workday. This odd, erratic occurrence was rare. But when it hit, I knew it to be useless to fight.

Getting home was my goal. Home to where my skittery condition could quench and dilute itself over some mindless activity. The trek there was slow, rush hour traffic crushing what little patience I had. About halfway to my destination, my mood morphed all on its own. To inveterate knowing. That feeling, the internal prompt, the unspoken voice that lifts its feather to my brain and challenges me to itch its tickle.

With little resistance, I pulled into the next strip mall and parked in the nearest spot. *I'm here, now what?* was my plea to the invisible pull on my actions. Looking across the storefronts, the one that caught my eye was one that sold videotapes (this being just before the downfall of the VCR), music, and electronics. I headed for the door and stepped inside. Toward the rear of the store, I could see a selection of books. Ahh, books. The uneasiness of my temperament vanished. In its place grew the promise of joy a new book always instilled in me.

I stood in front of the furthest back shelf taking in the oranges and blues, purples and maroons of the book spines. All calling me toward them. The freshly published fragrance caressing my smell. My emotional state completely transformed, I stepped forward to browse.

From near the bottom of the shelf a spine caught my eye. Lilac and whispering yellow in lined pattern, the rusty tangerine letters of its subtitle seducing my interest. Standing out in nonconformity to its neighbors. Shunning the vibrancy around it, it called to me. Transfixed my attention. I quickly forgot the glitter of bright promise the other books suggested and pulled it from the shelf.

The Highly Sensitive Person, by Dr. Elaine Aron. *How to Thrive When the World Overwhelms You.* This was it. My unspoken voice had spoken. My knowing quenched, the mission my day's long mood had sent me to find. A hole, decades in the making sending me its gratitude. I opened the book and flipped through it. Reading bits here and there. Every passage I hit squared with the oddities of my personality. Every quirk, every dip, every flaw, every question mark, every self-chastisement I owned. The model of human being God had made me into *did* have an instruction manual. And now I held it in my hands.

I raced to the checkout. I couldn't wait to get home to devour it.

Magdalena

When I was 18, my family took a trip to Montana to visit my mother's relatives. Our first stop was at my mother's oldest sister's house. Marianne was a joy to be around. Caring and kind, she wore her love for others on her face and throughout her body as if it were a permanent part of her attire.

I hadn't seen my aunt in some years, but I was surprised by her reaction to seeing me again. She gazed at me, as if mesmerized, through sparkling wetness. When she finally spoke, it was to my mother, "She is the spitting image of Magdalena," she said only glancing briefly at my mother.

"No," my mother was quick to say, "She resembles her, but I wouldn't say she is the spitting image of her."

I knew only little of Aunt Magdalena. She was the second oldest sister in my mother's large family and an intimate of Marianne's. At the time of Magdalena's death, Marianne was 19, married, and living with her husband. Magdalena at 17 had been very ill.

Like most of my mother's family at that time, Magdalena had been struck with an illness thought to be typhoid fever. As the story goes, seriously ill, Magdalena struggled to regain her health but was improving little by little. Until her fiancé visited her. He brought the news that he had found another love. And that he would soon marry the other woman.

Upon hearing the news, Magdalena lost all desire to fight. Within days, her health declined, and she finally succumbed to her disease.

Her cause of death, according to Marianne, was not typhoid fever, but a broken heart.

I listened intently to her two sisters argue back and forth about our resemblance. My mother was 5 years old at Magdalena's passing, but was sure she remembered more than my oldest aunt.

"Here, just a minute," Marianne said several minutes into the dispute. She sprung from her seat and retrieved a tattered and creased object from her closet. "See for yourself."

She didn't hand the object to my mother – she placed it in my hands. It was an old photograph. An ashen, jagged-edged portrait. Warped with many bends that had been smoothed flat over a period of decades. In my mother's household, like items were burned due to the typhoid, but Marianne's home was safe from such destruction. The photo survived as one of or the only remaining picture of Magdalena.

I sucked in my breath immediately upon seeing it. The object in my hands looked more like a mirror than a photograph. Marianne was right. The resemblance was unmistakable. We didn't just look like sisters, we looked like identical twins separated only by a fold of time – decades apart.

As eerie as that felt, I sensed something stronger. An

awareness of deep pain emanated from the picture. Not from her silhouette. She was the picture of health, smiling brightly and genuinely. The innocence of vibrant youth before tragedy.

The pain I absorbed seemed to float toward me like mist on a cool spring morning. It was a mix of melancholy love for the timbered mountainous country that surrounded us, the grief of separation from family, and a wound within the soul that agonizes beyond the words that describe love. These feelings permeated my skin, seeping deep within the cells of my body.

I palpated her broken heart. It beat within me. Slow and hobbled. Her begging heart wanted healing. Her begging eyes would not let me go.

"Let me see that," my mother whisked the photo from my hands breaking the bond that held me entrenched to it. After a moment of looking down at it, she claimed "I don't see it."

"Everyone we run into thinks Mom and I look exactly alike," I said to my aunt wanting to shove the anguished feeling from my core. If I pushed the conversation into another direction maybe I could sweep away the eeriness of its spell on me along with it.

Marianne nudged the beginning of a smile to her face as she accepted the photo back. Her eyes averted; their restraint avoided the search in mine. I bit the inside of my lip.

"Do you have a copy of that I can have?" I asked as nonchalantly as I could. Having held it in my hands I couldn't shake a kind of unbroken kinship with it.

"I'll make sure you get a copy," she said, her smile returning. Her mood more relaxed, it returned to its former tenderness.

<u>HSP Me</u>

I hadn't thought about Magdalena in years, but her

presence drifted in and amongst the words of Dr. Elaine Aron's book as I read that first night. Sifting into my awareness, her memory paralleled each new discovery I made of myself. As I paused to contemplate, the insight fell softly into place.

I thought about the phenomenon called limerence. That bizarre hold that unrequited love has on certain people. A life-or-death stranglehold. I suspected that my aunt was both highly sensitive and limerant over her young man. Magdalena's connection to me was more than familial. It was also relational through shared anomaly.

There were others like me. The book said so. But I knew, through that strange knowing that presented itself deep from within, of at least one. Though we never met, the communication was emotive. She spoke to me through my senses.

While thoughts of Magdalena distracted me, the book's greater impact held me spellbound. There was enough enlightening text in the book to describe my own personality. Simple quirks like why I felt so offended when my mother would tell me to stop being so sensitive. To the more important features of me like my strange relationship to fear in social interactions. Feeling overwhelmed in each new meeting. Comprehending nuances in a room of single people – who was interested in whom. After meeting a new man, reading the subtleties in his eyes. Feeling the intensity of biological urges, passion, affinity. As far back as high school, and the almost unbearable intensity of emotion I felt toward the young man in whom I had no more in common than a few shared experiences. For years I had called that experience limerence. Now I wondered if the two were somehow connected.

I thought about Louise and how similar Alice Miller's gifted child was to a highly sensitive person. Maybe even a precursor trait opening an avenue to exploitation.

I marveled at how on target each aspect of this individuality called highly sensitive person was. And it became clear how little people understood it. I didn't understand it and I was one. Up until now, I wasn't even aware of it as a difference in causation. I just thought *I* was weird. And that there was something wrong with me.

The reason I, and people like me, are different is because we have a different nervous system. I, and people like me, are just made differently. And up to 1 in 5 or 6 of us are like that. Not only are our reactions different, our perceptions, the way we see the world, is different. Which makes our experiences, perceptions, and inner lives unusual. Our reactions, according to most of the population, being unlike the norm, become absurd.

These differences come about because of different chemical responses. For instance, during stress HSPs' brains, according to the book, have been shown to contain more of two substances. Norepinephrine is associated with arousal. A kind of adrenaline for the brain. The other, cortisol, indicates that a person is basically in a constant state of arousal. This state can boot the fight or flight response into action rather quickly.

For the first time in 20 years, I could start to forgive myself for the way in which I interacted with my high school crush, with the musicians, with every potential romantic interest I'd ever met. I could forgive Cecilia for her belief that I was a *troubled* girl. Any person uneducated in this knowledge I now had would've come to the same conclusion. I myself did. Her perceptions of what was troubled and what was not didn't include a different way of perceiving. I could forgive my mother for her pleas to me to stop being so sensitive. She couldn't understand that it was an inherent part of who I am. She, like most everyone on the planet, had never imagined that my way of being was normal for someone whose nervous system was much more sensitive than her own. I could forgive. Both people in my life and myself. What a relief it was to forgive.

The book did not try to label sensitives as better than

others. On the contrary, they aren't better or worse and I was not better or worse. Just different. There were advantages to having a sensitive nervous system, and these were to be used to their fullest extent. And there were disadvantages. These disadvantages needed to be reframed and dealt with.

It was time to leave behind trying to fit my round hole persona into the square peg world surrounding me. Opening to my highly sensitive reality inspired new learning, new adventures, and the promise of experiences counter to the cookie cutter lives of women I had previously wanted to imitate.

Freedom

Freedom guides our actions in powerful ways. I hadn't been so much under the external control of other people as my own rigid belief system. The one that told me to conform to a set of rules I hadn't even thought through and honestly considered whether it was a good choice or not.

My third angel appeared at the right time to create a major turning point in my life. Providence had aligned to upend my flawed thinking. My prom dream of what I envisioned as a woman's typical progression through life was long gone. I was near 40 and hope of being a young bride was forever gone. I grieved that state of being. But coinciding with that feeling was a strange newness. A reborn kind of joy at being "different." I still wanted relationship. And the special relationship of marriage. But it no longer mattered like it had before. If I never married, I was okay with that. I could be myself.

People had accused me my whole life of being too sensitive. I was sensitive, but it wasn't a fault. It was a gift to be embraced. A gift that came with a warning that the world did not as yet understand those of us who were sensitives.

The question then became *How am I going to move forward in my life given this new knowledge?* For now, I decided, to simply be by myself, a joyous state that I'd learned sensitives crave for at least a part of each day. A craving I had long denied to myself. And I would do so for as long as I chose. I needed that time to think, to be, to contemplate. And in my unattached state, I had the freedom to do that.

The Cocoon

The time off I took after Mark had stretched to six months. In that time, much had happened. I had been introduced to the phenomenon of the Luna Moth, I'd changed careers, and I'd learned about being highly sensitive. The healing period had accomplished its purpose. I was ready to charge back into the social part of my life.

Years earlier when I was going to school to get my undergraduate degree, I'd met another tall woman at school one evening. She and I talked about a common problem we had. Meeting men who were willing to date a woman taller than themselves. It was comforting to commiserate with someone who experienced the same problems I had. We had both run into people who assumed tall women have more dates than they can handle, when the opposite was true. She handed me a business card for a club for tall singles, with the admonition to go where taller women found greater acceptance.

I had attended one gathering, but soon afterward had met Mark. I kept that card even though I had begun dating Mark. Now was the time, I decided, to search out that card and give it another try.

Romance, though, was not the biggest motivation to join. I wanted to enjoy the newly found freedom I'd just acquired. To enjoy the company of men while finding some women friends too. I had new strategies; those from the book, and ones I'd conjured up on my own. I was possessed with new adventure, and more confident than I had ever been fighting the social battle.

My first four months in the club were filled with different activities and getting acquainted with the members of the group. If I saw an attractive man, I would talk to him. But then I would move on. Intentionally I would move on. I was not going to allow myself to fall into any unrequited love. Memories of the happiness I felt with my first male friend, Wyn, fueled my drive to make that a priority. I still believed I could find a romantic partner who was also a friend. This was one of my approaches for dealing with the fight or flight issue that still plagued me.

I started having fun. Going to events, meeting people one-on-one. Or avoiding the crowds. Not going to an event because I felt more like being by myself. For the first time in a very long time, I was enjoying life to the fullest.

Metamorphosis

An office within the club came open. Social committee chair. Its duties were scheduling and putting together the social calendar. More specifically, organizing events and doing a monthly two-page spread for the newsletter letting everyone know when and where these events were held. Starting immediately, the office was to be occupied by two people as it had become a job too much for just one person. I decided it was time to start giving back and I applied for the job. Another woman and I got it.

The position seemed custom made for me. The other woman took on most of the duties of organizing the events, while I put together the write-ups and composed the layout for the newsletter. An outlet for creativity that was more enjoyable activity than it was a chore. We enjoyed working together, but it was still a large job. So much so we couldn't believe that the job had previously been successfully held by just one person.

One Saturday, I was feverishly working hard to get the layout done for the next month. The content was sparse for that month. The other woman and I had been exchanging calls trying to brainstorm some last-minute events to fill up the calendar. When the phone rang again, I assumed it was her.

"Hi, this is Anthony, from the tall club," the voice on the other end said.

"Oh, hi Anthony," I said curious why he was calling me. Anthony was 20-something, about 6'6", and a serviceman stationed in the area. He was a regular at the club.

"I heard you need some help doing the social calendar," he said, "I'd like to volunteer."

"Oh . . . fantastic," I said overjoyed, "We can use all the help we can get."

"Great," he said, "I'd love to help."

We added Anthony to our meetings.

The Butterfly

After Mark, I'd sheltered myself in a healing cocoon of solitude. Even as I ventured out into those first events, I had kept a serene distance between me and the obvious social nature of the group, preferring to flit from one person to the next. But the surface nature of that interaction was beginning to goad me with its shallowness. A position that left me feeling inauthentic. It was time to expose the real me.

I'd worked up to this night, I had to trust that my transformation was complete. It was time to spread my colorful wings to the wind. Allow my vulnerability to show and go deeper. This dance would be the test. My wings would either crumple and I would crash, or I would soar. Neither the dark and noisy hall nor the crush of people would keep me from this debut.

I stepped in the door and immediately took off to speak

to one of the more well-known and popular women in the group. Just a few minutes into our conversation, she pointed out a man across the room from us that I had never seen before.

"That's Bryce," she said, "He just broke up with Sandy."

Sandy was one of our members, a 6'3" or 6'4" beauty. I had met and talked with her before. But she was always alone. I'd never seen Bryce before.

"Mmm," I said.

"They were together two years," she continued. She looked over at me. Then smiled slyly. "You need to dance with him," she said as she raised her arm, motioning him toward us.

"What?" I said, "No, that's okay. Don't . . . "

I stopped mid-sentence as he got within a few feet of us.

She put a hand around his upper arm and introduced us.

"I think you should dance with Bryce," she said pushing me toward him, "Go on . . ."

My face reddened in the darkness. He was a very attractive man. Taller than most of our group. At 6'9", he made me feel short.

I looked into Bryce's eyes expecting that he too was feeling embarrassed at her obvious prompting. He returned my look with a playful smile. "Sure, why not?" he said, nodding toward the dance floor with his eyes still on mine.

"Okay, "I said brushing away as much of the discomfort as I could. We danced a slow dance, and I very much enjoyed it. But being determined not to focus on one man for the entire evening, I left him with a smile and a "thank you for the dance."

I drifted around the perimeter watching people enjoying themselves. I didn't feel out of place here. The way I did outside this bubble. The world beyond seemed so out of sync with my rhythms. The church singles' events, the few singles' gatherings at the silk stocking law firm I'd spent years working for. These groups always left me feeling like an interloper. Trespassing on their clan. Here we shared a common bond, and I was part of that whole. Accepted.

As I noticed these thoughts going through my mind, I could feel a pair of eyes on me. I had seen Dean before at different events but had never spoken to him. "Hi," I said acknowledging his gaze, "I'm Monica."

We talked for a short period of time. After 20 minutes or so of talking, I began to feel the crush of overwhelm. Over stimulation in a highly sensitive person. Since reading Elaine Aron's life manual for HSPs, I'd begun to recognize the feeling. And label it. As comfortable as I felt in this environment, I tired very easily of the noise and chi-chat. Over stimulation had set in. It was time to go home.

The Love Conundrum

Love is something we all want. It is the facilitator to the ultimate human goal of self-realization. I'd come to recognize that the opposite of love is not hate. The opposite of love is fear. Although love is a powerful and desirable force, it is also a gentle force. Like water trickling over a stone to smooth its edges.

Fear is a brutal force. A bully. Left to its own devices, it can subvert love. Capable of pushing its way over love and stomping it to pieces.

For an HSP, any emotion is strongly and deeply felt. Fear is a tormentor for people with conventional limbic systems. But it is an oppressive dictator for an HSP. When I realized this axiom, it became even more important to me to find a way to cope with the fear that surrounded any feelings I might develop for a man.

I was sure this was the mistake I made with my high school crush, excluding all others, focusing on him alone. Fear won. I wondered too if it wasn't a factor for Dante, the musician, and our failure to connect. If true, fear on both sides prevented any chance for a relationship to germinate. Another victory for fear. It, I decided, had dominated far too long. It was time for fear to go down in flames.

Practice and confrontation were my answers. Confront my fears. Force myself to talk to people. With each interaction, I would have to get better.

The second part of the plan was a little bit trickier. Dealing with the possibility of too strong and intense feelings far too soon. First, I determined to become succinctly aware of every feeling that surfaced. Then, I resolved to confront any feelings that might develop, accept them for what they were, and reassure myself that they were normal. But I also was not going to latch onto one man, heaping all my love energy on him to the dismissal of any other possibility. At least until I had some reassurance of a return of my affection.

Biological Gravity

I've always found gravity to be an interesting concept. You can't feel it. Physically. But its presence plays a big part in our lives. Its simplest explanation is the force that attracts two bodies toward each other. And it explains everything from why objects roll downhill to why the planets in our solar system circle the sun.

There is another force of nature equally compelling. It does the same thing – attracts two bodies toward each other. In this case, it is two human bodies. It is the biological force of attraction. This is a more selective force. It doesn't work on everyone at once. It chooses its targets at random and strikes each duo homing in on them with universal exclusivity. There is no escape from its all-encompassing power.

If you doubt gravity's power, try jumping up in the air as high as you can get. Before you know it, you will come down. That's gravity working its magic. Biological attraction has that same invisible yet intransigent force. It had been years since I'd experienced its full pull. In fact, I had almost come to believe that it was a youthful phase that I just grew out of. That is until one chilly evening in March.

I had been looking forward to this night. It was the Miss Tall pageant in our city. The reason for my interest was not because I was competing. But because every woman I knew in the club was competing. And there were many men planning to attend. Ideal conditions for a captive audience, if not a one-sided one. In my favor.

I got to the door where a gentleman I recognized but barely knew was taking tickets and tearing them in half. He was an accountant whom I'd met once before. He had a friendly smile and easy demeanor. "Enjoy," he said as he handed me back my half ticket.

Turning around I nearly ran directly into the man in line behind me. He was even taller than the average male in our group. A perfect 7 inches taller than myself. With blond hair and dappled blue eyes, the color of a cerulean sunset. He wore a warm smile.

"Excuse me," I said as I tried to slip past his gravitational energy.

Upon entering the hall, I could see men everywhere. I scanned the room for someone to talk to. My eyes fell upon Dean. He was surrounded by several other men in deep conversation.

I walked over and joined their circle. As I listened to the dialogue, I could sense someone's eyes upon me. I glanced in that direction and saw the blue-eyed man from the ticket line. He was looking intently at me. I could feel the corner of my mouth move gently upward into a slight smile as I realized the attraction must be mutual.

Maybe I will find a way to introduce myself to him tonight, I thought. Before I finished that thought, he'd walked the forty or so feet from the back of the room and was now walking by our little cluster. He caught Dean's eye as he got closer, and Dean greeted him.

Dean looked at me and said, "Monica, this is Jim. Jim Nelson."

<u>Joke Party</u>

When I was a teenager, I loved to free-form dance. I'd put on an album of folk music and with my limited dance floor of whatever open space the living room provided, I'd sail from corner to corner, moving my entire body to the rhythms. Losing myself in the music, I'd move in flow knowing instinctively what my next flourish would be.

Nothing I did was choreographed. I simply felt what my next move would be. Joy leading my limbs. The freedom was bliss. The movement a silencing of my inner turmoil.

This release conflicted with the detailed scripting of how I wanted my life to progress. I only indulged in a rare private moment. I thought that if I were ever to be happy, I would have to plan and execute the path I believed would take me to my goal. No free movement was allowed.

Part of this aim for my life had been who I would choose as a life partner for myself. I had definite desire that led me. Drove me toward that person. And I would accept that instinctual drive as my destiny. Work toward that intention. Hold onto the objective with determination.

Twenty, or thereabouts, years into my adult life, I realized the futility of defining every detail of my life. So often, it hadn't progressed like I would've liked. And the striving, the disappointments, the heartbreak was overwhelming me. I longed for the peace of mind my younger days' free-form dance gave my mind. It was with this mindset that I found myself on the evening of this intimate gathering.

It was a crisp spring temperature. The sky only starting to reveal its starry splendor. My mood seemed to blend with the romantic feel of nature. The peace and calm that can only come from something beyond yourself.

I hadn't been to an event for a while. At times, it was more than I could face, all the social interaction. But I decided to go to this one. It was a smaller gathering at one of our member's home, where people were instructed to bring jokes or riddles to share. I thought it might be interesting, and I ventured out.

When I got there, I was relieved to see that it was an even smaller gathering than I expected. The home where it took place had a living room that connected to a larger open space with a fireplace. The living area had a couple couches and chairs surrounding a coffee table. Even more chairs had been added to the circle to accommodate the gathering. I chose a spot on one of the couches and took some deep breaths.

It was an atmosphere that was more conducive to more intimate talk. Maybe one of the men I was becoming attracted to would be there – Dean or Bryce or even the newest man I'd met, Jim. There was also a man I'd seen before but had never talked to sitting by the fireplace. He had been part of a couple who had recently broken up. As I took my seat on the couch, I could feel his eyes following me.

Erica, a woman I knew and liked from the club who also happened to be the pageant winner, entered the door and we said "hello" from across the room. I liked Erica. She was an inch taller than I was and very vivacious. She moved on to the kitchen where some people were putting snacks out.

I scanned the room taking in the atmosphere, warm and serene. My eyes skimmed the door just as it opened. It was Jim. He had a folder under his arm with dog-eared papers randomly jammed into a folder and a pocketful of pens. I smiled to myself. He looked like a geek. I loved geeks. I considered myself one in high school. I understood them, not like the popular guys I'd seen there, whose behavior seemed incomprehensible. (As a junior in high school, there was a well-liked football player who chose to sit next to me in Geometry. He openly admitted to me that he selected that seat so he could copy my work. It unnerved as well as baffled me that he would reveal this to me.)

Jim came into the circle in the living room and sat at a 45-degree angle to me. We spoke briefly before the party and joke-telling began. I didn't really have any jokes to share – I'd come to listen. Jim had many to relate. He pulled out e-mail after e-mail of anecdotes and memes. Some hilariously funny, others smile-worthy only. I listened intently to every word, but if you asked me to repeat them, I wouldn't have been able to.

After the joke-telling part of the night ended, he got up and left for the kitchen. I sat for a while in the quiet of the enclosed seating area. Everyone had left but me. After a few minutes of solitude and sheltering alone time, I ambled off to the kitchen in hopes of being able to talk to him. Erica and he were huddled in a doorway talking. I stood around by the bar for a few minutes looking over the snacks. Then, I moved around a bit talking briefly to different people. Returning to the kitchen, they were still talking. I walked up to both and said "hi." We three talked briefly. When it became apparent, Erica was not going anywhere I drifted off. Maybe I would find the guy by the fireplace and introduce myself. I looked around – he was gone.

I glanced one more time into the kitchen. Erica was gone, but I did not see Jim either. Maybe it was time for me to leave also. I said my goodbye to the hostess and left.

I was almost to my car when Jim jumped in beside me. He surprised me, appearing out of the shadows.

"Hi," he said, "I thought you'd never leave."

"What?" I giggled, "I wanted to talk to you, but you were spending a lot of time with Erica."

I couldn't believe I was talking to him in this way. Being so blunt and to the point had gotten me into trouble before. But he seemed comfortable. And not adversely affected by it. Like we had been old friends forever.

We stopped walking simultaneously. "You were always talking to someone new. I didn't have a chance," he said.

I wrinkled my forehead remembering all my alone time, "No, you were the one always occupied."

"Okay, whatever," he said, "talk to me now."

We did the whole *what do you do?* thing, amongst other superficial talk. When there was a pause in the conversation, we looked at one another. I decided to venture out a little. "So, are you planning to go dancing?" There was a scheduled get-together at a nightclub in the upcoming weekend.

He looked thoughtful for a moment. "I don't know," he said. "Maybe. I don't like to dance."

"You should come," I said, "I'm planning on going."

"We'll see," he said. "Are you leaving now?"

"Yes," I said, "It's getting late."

He continued looking into my eyes. That biological gravity refused to let go. I swore I could see the blue of his eyes in the starlight, but darkness enfolded the both of us. "Good night," I said, pushing at my hesitation, hoping to make my legs move. It took an act of will. But in adopting a freeform attitude toward my future required surrender in every little detail. Staying longer might've caused me to fall into the trap of falling too fast, too soon. I turned and left.

<u>Will he Show?</u>

I didn't really want to go to this nightclub event. I wasn't in the mood to go out that night. But I had told Jim that I would be there, so I knew I couldn't write it off.

I got there early and found a coveted close-in parking spot. Close to downtown, this new nightclub had made a strategic mistake in not acquiring enough space to provide adequate parking. I was the first person from our club to get there so I gathered several tables together, enough for the expected turnout. Too many, as it turned out.

I sat for a good half hour before anyone from our group showed. Over the next two hours only four or five more people joined our group. Apparently, everyone else had the same sense of just not wanting to go out this night. Or had other plans.

I intermittently joined the group chitchat, while keeping my eye on the entrance door. Jim was nowhere to be found. Around 10:30 I decided I'd had had enough. I was sure he wasn't going to show. I said my good-byes and left.

Walking outside I was almost to my car when I saw Jim walking up the street. I waited next to my door watching him watching me.

"Are you leaving?" he said as he got closer.

"Yes, it was kind of a bust. Not many people came. Not a lot of fun." I smiled a sarcastic smile.

"I guess I won't stay then, I'm parked in a no parking zone," he threw his head in the direction of the street we were on.

We both looked down the street where a police officer was beginning the long descent down the road writing out tickets.

"You want to go get something to eat?" he said turning back toward me.

"Sure," I said, glad he wanted to continue our conversation. "Maybe you better drive?" I grinned a little too broadly as we both continued to watch law enforcement at work.

"Yeah," he said, "let's go."

It's sometimes advantageous to have long legs, I thought as we hoofed it toward his car, reaching our destination with a three-vehicle buffer.

A First Date

We went to an overnight diner. The intent was to get breakfast.

Our waitress was a young girl no more than seventeen, with piercings all over her body, the most prominent of which was a small diamond that looked like it was glued to her chest right where a princess-length chain's pendant might fall.

His brow wrinkled slightly as a look of curiosity ran across his eyelids. I put a finger to my lip to stop any embarrassing involuntary reaction.

We both folded our menus and handed them back to her.

"I'll just have hot tea," I said.

Jim echoed me with a request for hot tea also.

As our waitress turned to leave, he bent forward. With playfulness in his voice, he said, "Do you think that hurts?"

"You mean all those piercings?" I asked.

"Especially that one just below her neck," he said. "How does it stay in place?"

"I have no idea . . . can't even imagine," I said. Giggling to myself, I silently contemplated how old I'd gotten in the blink of an eye.

"Why do people do that to themselves?"

"I think it's a young person's thing," I said.

Talking to Jim was surprisingly easy. I felt like we'd known each other for many years. After breaking the ice discussing our waitress's body jewelry, we got down to the business of getting to know one another. We spent a good hour in conversation. I knew more about him than many of the men I'd dated before. I felt I'd learned more about his character in one hour than I had ever learned about Mark in the seven years we'd been together.

As we realized it was time to end our date, a seriousness fell across his face. "I have to tell you something," he said.

"O . . . kay," I said drawing out the word slowly and

deliberately.

"I'm married," he said without blush or hesitation, "We're separated. But I'm not divorced . . . just yet."

"Oh," I said trying not to sound too disappointed. This possibility didn't occur to me. The tall club was a singles' group and I assumed that everyone was *single*. The assumption seemed appropriate to me. "Thanks for telling me."

He dropped me off next to my car, jumped out and walked me to my door.

"I enjoyed this," he said, "Can we do it again?"

I turned from my door to face him. "I can't," I said, struggling for the right thing to say, "I won't date anyone who is married."

"I understand," he said looking down into my eyes.

I didn't want him to misunderstand. I enjoyed his company immensely. The communication was exactly as I had envisioned a relationship to be. Something missing in my relationship with Mark. It was the stuff of lasting pairings. The stuff I'd found so elusive for the first forty years of my life.

"I'd like to be friends," I said hoping what I'd just said didn't sound as cliché as the words themselves were bound to be. I really did want to continue a friendship. "You'll still come to the Tall Club, right?"

"Yes," he said turning to go back to his car, "We'll see each other again."

Chapter 10 - Coming Together

Brain Civil War

Down through the centuries, poets, novelists and composers have all tried to define what romantic love is. How it works. What it does to people. To explain the drive itself. What has resulted is a confluence of description that is true from the originator's standpoint, but only part of a massive, larger truth. Yet a succinct portrayal remains elusive. The experience is unique from the perspective of the lover.

Neuroscience has now begun to study what happens to drive one sex toward another, one individual to another, in the act we call romantic love. Their initial findings are not as sentimental as the artists' renderings.

These findings as described in *The Chemistry Between Us*, by Larry Young, PhD. And Brain Alexander, reveal that it is all very mechanical. The process begins -- where else? -- in the sympathetic nervous system as arousal. This is not sexual arousal as we commonly perceive it. But a general state of arousal. We experience an urge, stirring an appetite. The appetite seeks reward. Sensing the appetite is well and good for a while, but eventually the person experiencing it will want consummation.

Appetite can come in many forms. When the form is sexual appetite, the limbic system (and hypothalamus) steps in to forge us ahead with our quest for consummation. If all our brain was made up of limbic system alone, we'd act without thought – flirting, fighting, unaware and cavalier in our hunt to satisfy our desires. The "bottom" portion of our brains the culprit for instigating this behavior.

Fortunately for our survival and vital to our need for a civilized society, another part of our brain steps in at this point. The "top" portion of our brains (the medial preoptic area, nucleus accumbens, amygdala and VTA) acts like the authoritative parent to the unruly child of the bottom brain. These components are responsible for weighing options, accounting for consequences, making good choices.

The two portions of the brain work together to progress the species while at the same time ensure that we do it in a civilized way. The system nature built into us works well most of the time. But it can cause conflict. Much like the conflict of mind I experienced with my allegiance to my summer friend vs. my own desire for her lost admirer.

As I got older and more experienced in the ways of life, I became better at confronting the excitability of my enhanced limbic system. Especially when it came to men. The two portions of my brain worked together more harmoniously. The better I got at this, the more comfortable I became with men. And, as an added benefit, the more comfortable they became with me.

Cookbook Wars

I had gotten to this tall club event early. My cohorts on the social committee and I were hoping this would be a well-attended event. It was a fundraiser for the group. An auction. People had donated certain items. We were going to auction them off. And the proceeds were to benefit the group. Following the auction, we would have a short social time.

Between helping set up, I mulled over the items up for auction. Nothing particularly grabbed me until I spied a past fundraising item. It was a cookbook compiled with recipes from tall clubs across the country. A purple-covered, spiral bound book jam-packed with various club members' favorite recipes. I stopped what I was doing to scan through the book. This, I thought, was what I wanted. I could see myself going home with it.

I felt eyes on me as I flipped the last pages. I looked up to see Jim across the room. As our eyes met, I smiled and inched my hand into a shy wave.

Our appointed auctioneer was standing at his podium, and at that moment, he raised his voice, "Let's find a seat. We need to get started."

Jim sat down in a chair at the back. I took a seat three-quarters of the way down on the opposite side. Throughout the start of the auction, I was very much aware of his presence behind me. I sensed he was aware of mine.

I was so preoccupied with him behind me that I missed the initial call for the cookbook I wanted. It seemed no one wanted it. The first bid, a very small one, brought me back to the auction environment and my determination to go home with the cookbook.

"Five dollars," I said firmly.

From the back of the room, I heard a male voice. "Six."

I turned to look. It was Jim holding up his arm. *What does he want with that cookbook?* I thought.

Someone else had bid seven, then seven-fifty. The book garnered more interest than I thought it would with its hesitative beginning.

"Ten." By now, I didn't have to look, I knew he was doing the bidding.

"Eleven," I said even more determined.

"Twelve," was his quick reply.

Okay, I thought, my mood hitting stubborn, *If you want a war, bring it on*. It was down to who could last longest. No one else was bidding. I had to finish this.

"Fifteen," I said sure he would see I meant business and back down.

I watched the faces of everyone around us swivel like they were at Wimbledon. All eyes were on him.

He grinned. "Twenty."

Everyone turned to look at me. My stubbornness faded. No matter how much I wanted that cookbook, I was not going to venture past twenty dollars for it. A wave of disappointment hit me. I hesitated, thinking it over. It occurred to me that I'd seen another one floating around the table. Maybe I still had the chance to go home with it.

Looking into the auctioneer's eyes, I slowly shook my head from side to side. He took the cue and said, "Sold," pointing to Jim.

After the auction I decided I would do a little friendly teasing. Rub it in a bit. He deserved it, I reasoned, going after what I wanted. I'd thrown a monkey wrench into it though because there *was* another cookbook that was eventually auctioned, and I walked away with it for seven dollars.

Holding my newly purchased prized possession, I walked over to Jim.

"Okay there, Mr. Ruthless," I said, "I got my cookbook for a bargain compared to yours. What do you say to that?"

He smiled sweetly and said, "I'm disappointed. I bought this for you. But you had to go and get that one."

Stunned, my mouth fell open. My mind went blank. He had successfully blind-sided me.

"Uhhhhh," I stammered. Feeling the pressure to say something, I finally said the first thing that came to me. "What am I going to do with two copies of the same cookbook?"

With a devilish grin, he pushed the book toward me, "You'll figure it out."

Resume Help

Jim was looking for a new job. We had run into each other at another social gathering and got to talking about resumes. He was frustrated with his. It was long and unwieldy. He had so much experience with so many things over a period of decades. He was now struggling to condense and summarize it to maximum impact.

I was excited. I loved taking information in its most raw form and molding it into a concise form of communication.

One of the most desirable aspects of my undergraduate work was the fact that the school I attended required at least one term paper written in every single class. This included my accounting and finance classes. I looked forward to that assignment and I was good at it too. I'd also moved on from computer programming. I hated writing code – so analytical and left-brained. I wanted to be free to sculpt communication. Not to have to stay within the confines of acceptable phrases. I was now working as a technical writer. Molding thought into language that conveyed a specific and unique meaning was true self-expression. To me, this was art at its finest.

I could hardly contain my excitement. "I would love to help you with that," I said with the energy of growing delight.

"Okay," he said, "I need to write it myself. It is my resume, but we can talk about it."

"Yes, yes," I said backing down a little on my enthusiasm. He was right. It had to be his work. It wouldn't be proper for me, as much as I would love to do it, to write it for him. "Of course."

"Here" he said, pulling out a piece of paper and scribbling a phone number on it, "I'm staying at my parents' house for now. Give me a call sometime and we'll talk."

I called him a few days later. We spent two hours on the phone, but after my initial stated reason for making the call, neither one of us mentioned the resume. This phone call started a ritual of evening phone conversations. Twice or three times a week, sometimes four, he would call me after dinner, and we would spend hours talking. Sometimes until 2:00 or 3:00 in the morning.

Starting to Date Again

It was time. I'd had my healing period after Mark. I'd had that much needed alone time. I was ready to start dating again. I wasn't sure how I would go about it, but I was ready to have a new relationship.

As Jim and I continued our marathon phone conversations, we began building a strong emotional bond. I'd never before met a man that I felt I could discuss intimate subjects with. Our conversations were long and philosophical.

The friendship we were building was deepening. But I was also feeling something stronger. The stronger feeling made me nervous. I was afraid I was falling in love. His marital status was changing but hadn't changed yet, and I certainly didn't want to fall too soon, as I had in the past.

So, I was quite pleased when I answered the phone one day to learn it was Dean calling. He asked me if I wanted to go on a drive to the mountains with him the following Saturday. I was still attracted to Dean and I liked him too. Before I met Jim, I hoped one day to have a chance to go out with Dean. He never seemed interested in more than friendship. Until now.

He picked me up early afternoon and we drove for hours, talking, listening to music, and stopping occasionally to take in the view. It was a pleasant and relaxed time.

After several hours and as we headed back, I felt happy. It had been an enjoyable date. I liked him and thought I would go out with him again should he ask. But I was also feeling like I was ready to call the date over. There arose in me a need for solace. That craving for alone time that I was beginning to acknowledge within myself and not ignore.

Visions of years earlier with my encounter with the first musician, David, surfaced. I was approaching that kind of uncomfortable state. I didn't understand it then. I was beginning to realize it now. Since then, I had learned that alcohol was a trigger for overstimulation in an HSP. Alcohol wasn't a problem anymore – migraine was an effective deterrent for that. But I had deduced that the situation with David went further than just alcohol overstimulation. At that time, and now, I figured out that "putting my best foot forward" when spending time with a new romantic interest was also a means of overstimulation to my nervous system.

I was newly aware of this trait in me but not practiced in making those closest to me aware of it.

As we approached the edge of town, Dean turned to me and asked if I was hungry. I hesitated. I was but was also more than ready to go home.

"My friends are having a dinner party tonight. Come with me," he said.

I hesitated. "I'm really kind of tired. I think I'd like to go home," I said. Tired wasn't the best descriptor of how I felt but I could not come up with something closer to the truth on such short notice.

His smile dropped, and his eyes fell in sync with them. "They'd really love to meet you. Please come with me."

His voice had almost a pleading quality to it and the weight of his eagerness surrounded me piercing my chest.

"Okay," I said giving into the tug, "I guess that would be alright."

I knew it was a mistake immediately, but I had already agreed. Adding a houseful of people I didn't know to my already overstimulated state only made me feel worse. His friends were gregarious, outgoing and very welcoming of me. A state most people find pleasant and embracing. But their targeted attention to me, uncomfortable by itself, only added to my need for solitude.

When Dean asked me to take a walk with him after dinner, I jumped at the chance to get some fresh air and distance. We walked along a landscaped path into a lovely garden area. I was content ambling gently along, smelling the fragrance of nature, until he stopped. I looked at him and he leaned in and kissed me.

Three hours earlier it would've been a welcome gesture at my back door. Now it was just one more thing. One more stressor to an already accentuated state of mind. What I now was beginning to recognize as overstimulation of my nervous system.

I paused, contemplating several different responses. I didn't want to hurt his feelings, but I had reached my limit. "I've had a lovely time today, Dean," I said, "But I would like to go home now."

His eyes pleaded with my words. "But it's not late at all . . ."

"Please," I said, and more under my breath, " . . . understand."

I wanted to explain it. What seemed like a frazzled state percolating within me. Forcing my thoughts and being into a hypervigilant state. To make him understand it wasn't him. Simply me, who I was. Any words that came to mind were inadequate.

"Okay," he said. The tone of dejection in his voice rubbing against my guilt zones.

I'd given in once to the impulse his manner requested of me. But I was also trying to do what was right for me. I was breaking new ground. In the years since Louise, I'd fought the daily battle of asserting my needs. Now on the wobbly legs of new-found confidence in this most recent knowledge about myself and my sensitive nature, the battle found new ground. I had to stand up for my needs even if it meant that the man I was with would not accept it.

Still, it wasn't fair to ask someone to accept this difference in me if I couldn't explain it adequately. I had more work to do.

The Start of One Popular Week

My date with Dean was the beginning to one standout week in my life. Throughout my dating history, a period of close to twenty years, dates were sparse. I'd even had some periods where I'd gone years without having one date. Expectation from this past behavior told me to savor the date

I'd had with Dean because it would be a long time before another one. And I did. The yearning for solitude waned after I finally got home and spent the next day alone by myself. In its place, the warmth from the enjoyable parts of our date returned. A date high.

This was the contentment I'd come to appreciate. I was used to stretching this contentment into months and years if necessary. I didn't know if he would want a second date. I felt like he liked me enough to want one, but I couldn't always tell. In the meantime, I would return to my life as it was.

Jim called the Monday following. I always looked forward to our phone calls. As I got to know Jim, I discovered something remarkable about him. Every man I had met up until this time seemed fragile to me. Frightened, or intimidated. Even Dean seemed aloof. I had sunk into the perspective that men were just that way. That there was no man willing to take the risk of rejection. And I was sure my sensitive vibes didn't help.

Jim was not like that. I knew from our talks that he was different when it came to risks. He had already acted sooner than most men. I'd learned much about him. He spent his life until he met me stepping out into the unknown. Jumping out of airplanes in the Air Force. Driving race cars for fun and profit. And eagerly running toward and into the eye of dangerous weather as a ham radio storm spotter when most sane people were hiding in their basements. And, above all, he wasn't afraid to befriend me, even if it meant that that was all we could be was friends. I always hung up the phone with that same feeling of warmth.

This night was different. Our conversation started out as it usually did, quickly moving from the more superficial to deeper subjects. But he seemed preoccupied, that distraction stretching out through the telephone lines and touching my senses.

"What is it?" I said. "You seem to have something on

your mind?"

"I do," he said.

I waited. He would tell me. I didn't have to prompt him.

"There's something different about you," he said. "You're not like other women."

"What is different?" I said. I grappled between unnerved and just curious. *Different* was not girlfriend material. Different was *different*. It usually meant "Monica the Mongoose," or "I'd ask you out if you weren't so damn tall." Or worse of all, "too sensitive."

"You talk about things that are deeper than the everyday crap most people talk about."

"What do you mean? Everyday crap," I said as I relaxed a little. It was half question, half exclamation mark. "You have to talk about everyday sometimes. It's survival." Maslow's triangle and its implications had been the subject of more than one of our conversations.

"Yeah," he paused, "but you wouldn't believe the dumb shit that comes from some people. You'd think they didn't have a brain."

He was saying he liked my brain. It was a compliment of the highest reaches.

"I learn from you," he went on.

"I learn from you too," I said.

"It's something I'd like to be around. All the time."

A Date a Quarter-Century Later

The day following my conversation with Jim, the climate was damp and gray. But the atmosphere did not pull my mood down with it. It was a new situation for me – this mutual chemistry. I allowed myself a little levity. To float amongst my happiness.

Running a little late, I had to leap toward and through the door to the shuttle bus that would take me to within yards of my workplace's front door. As the door closed, the edge of my black raincoat's tail centered itself within the folds of the now latched doors. I gave it a slight tug to release it.

As I moved my glance from the newly released fabric to the bus's interior, I met Bryce's gaze. It would've been hard to miss him on this bus. Standing hunched over in the back, head skimming the ceiling, his eyes latched onto mine as I glided down the walkway. I slid into an open space next to him. As the bus jostled and swayed, we talked, laughing at the harmonic way the bus threw us about. The synchronized nature of our movements in flow to the bus's jarring. As my stop approached, I offered up my parting good-byes.

"Hey," he said, "How about lunch?" He nodded toward the food court across the street from where the bus sat momentarily paused. "About noon? I'll meet you in front."

The content of my talk with Jim was still percolating through my mind. New and yet to reach its final form. This synergy lay over the backdrop of my *keep an open mind* policy. Jim and I were not yet a couple though I felt we might soon be. I didn't have much time to contemplate before the bus closed its door on my choice.

"Yeah, okay. See you at 12:00," I said, barely slipping through the closing escape hatch.

The food court was always a crowded venue. A dozen miniature versions of typical fast-food eateries lining the perimeter of a sprawling and congested middle section. A spanning ooze of noisy ultra-rushed professionals with chowhound mentality. I tried to breathe. We nudged our way through the crowd.

After getting our food, we secured a barren spot amidst the melee. As we sat, Bryce began talking in an easy and confident manner.

He told me about his early life. Where he went to high school, playing basketball for his hometown team. The town he grew up in was just down the highway from mine. I couldn't recall ever seeing him at a basketball game, though my school played his. But I couldn't be expected to remember, I told myself, since it had been so many years. He'd gotten an athletic scholarship to college and attended about two years before an injury sidelined him.

This topic interested me. In the beginning. But when I tried to move into deeper subjects, he would return to basketball. With a renewed effort I tried to recall what I knew about the game, from my teenage spectator days in the pep band and playing on Wyn's team just barely into my adult life. It was clear Bryce was an expert on the subject. I felt I had little to contribute to the conversation.

Our lunch nearly done, he paused momentarily. I searched my numb mind for a new topic, but silence prevailed in the breath between. As I opened my mouth to say something, anything, he aroused a new subject with similar passion. Cars. I pushed back on my chair in silent sigh. Another subject I knew little about. Enough to know when to take my car into the shop and that was about all.

I set my intention to 100% listen mode, but I had a difficult time keeping it focused. My mind wandered to Jim and the talks that we had. He was intelligent and well-read. I always came away from our conversation with new insights, and the stimulation of intellectual conversation. But I also felt free to talk about subjects of which I knew more than he did. Jim was neither intimidated nor dismissive. Our talks were not just intellectual, they were intimate. He did not back off from telling me his feelings – sharing his deepest desires, ambitions, and goals. Even the painful emotions – broken dreams, sorrows, hurts – he shared with me.

"I need to get back to work," I said as the food court residents began to shuffle out, "the attorneys don't take kindly to their staff taking long lunches." It was a truth, they didn't. But I was aware too that this was a rule I might be inclined to break and take the consequences for if it was Jim sitting opposite me.

As I returned to the office, the impression of my date with Bryce sent my mind looking to evaluate the last hour. My imagination fought for a positive basis on which to justify the time. It came to me in a quiet flash.

It may have taken twenty-five years, but I finally had the high school date that I had longed so heartily for all those years past. Back then, I would've been so pleased to sit spellbound with a guy and listen to him talk about basketball and cars. Not only did it feel lifeless to me now, but experiencing this date seemed to set Jim even further apart from the crowd.

And Another One

I was only midway through my popular week when I picked up the phone to a voice I was unfamiliar with. A polite and soft-spoken gentleman, he introduced himself to me as the ticket taker at the door the night I first met Jim. I didn't recall having spoken to him since that night and I was immediately curious why he was on the phone. Maybe, my first thought landed softly, he wanted to add something to this month's social calendar.

Gently, but with a strong confidence, he asked if I would be willing to go out on a date with him. My mouth didn't want to work, which didn't seem to matter as I had no words crawling out of the jumble going through my mind.

He was patient and waited for me to say something. I forced my mind through the jumble. The list with all its details forming in my mind. Jim in the forefront. Dean still appearing. Bryce having just recently dropped off. Did I want to add one more to this overwhelm of interest?

"I'm sorry," I finally said, "That would be nice, but I've just started dating someone exclusively."

It wasn't true. I was far from being in an exclusive

relationship. Though I'd hoped that Jim's admission might turn into exclusivity, I wasn't yet ready to own it.

But I knew within me where I wanted the future to go. I much preferred the quiet of a one-on-one to the multiplicity of the previous week. The anxiety of trying to juggle so many interests was exhausting. So, I reasoned to myself, the lie was not such a bad one. Besides, I felt certain I knew where I was headed now. But he was such a nice man, it seemed the best way to avoid hurting his feelings.

"Thank you," his voice was still pleasant and genial, "I just had to ask."

Hanging up the phone, my mood downshifted abruptly. He was so cordial and sweet. A swell of feeling thumped slowly against my heart. Rejection, loneliness, guilt. The feelings collided. I couldn't separate the intermingling conglomerate. They weren't all mine. I knew that. But they swelled inside of me as if they were.

Maybe it was a good thing that I was never very popular. I certainly didn't like the feelings created when I turned someone down.

Buy A Dinner

Popularity grew another ugly head as I faced a new quandary. We had an unusual kind of social event coming up at the tall club. And I didn't know what to do.

Jim and I had talked since his admission to me a couple of weeks earlier, but we carefully avoided saying any more about it. Even though I had only had one date with Dean, I still wasn't ready to close off that avenue altogether yet. I knew I had to face down the uncertainty, make the hard choice, and move forward. For my sake, as well as the two gentlemen involved.

This event and the conflict it presented came at the wrong time. I was still mulling over every detail of the choice ahead of me.

It was a rare kind of event we were having. The men from the group were supposed to bring a full dinner that they had prepared. Then that dinner would be auctioned to the highest bidder. Women were in the role of buyer. The winner of each meal then would enjoy eating that dinner with the man who brought it.

My conundrum was that Dean and Jim might both be there. I didn't want to be forced into that decision yet.

Jim brought up the subject of the dinner in one of our conversations. He told me he was bringing roast chicken. Did I like that?

"Yes," I said, "Sounds good. You'll probably get lots of bidders."

"Are you going to bid on it?" he said.

"Um," I wasn't sure what to say. After an uncomfortable silence, I said, "I'm not sure I'm going to go."

"Why not?" If there was one trait about Jim I had learned and learned well, it was that he was very direct. He wasn't afraid to say or ask anything.

"I just don't know if I want to go," I said hoping he would just drop it.

"You need to go and bid on my dinner," he teased, "I'm making it for you."

"Oh," I said, "Don't do that. Make what you want. Just enjoy the evening. I'm sure you'll have lots of bids."

"No, no," he said, his tone taking on a more serious inflection, "I want to have dinner with you."

I laughed. "Okay, we'll see," I said. I wanted to have dinner with Jim, but I didn't want to hurt Dean's feelings if he were to show up. The pressure of my decision weighing on me, maybe I should make it now, I thought.

As the day approached, I took up the idea again with no solution in sight. I just couldn't go. I was not ready.

I spent the evening at home alone. At about 10:30, Jim

called.

"Where were you?"

"I told you I didn't feel like going." I couldn't tell him the reason I didn't want to go was because I was afraid that I might hurt another man's feelings.

"I made this dinner for you and you didn't come," I could tell he was back to teasing me.

"So how was it? The event." I said.

"It was a bust. No one came. Only a few people."

"Oh, that's too bad," I said. Maybe I wasn't the only one who felt uncomfortable with the idea.

"We decided not to do the auction," he continued, "We just set everything out potluck style and made it a group thing."

"Really?" I said, "Who all was there?"

Jim named off the short list of attendees. Dean was not one of them. I could've gone.

"Is that all?"

"Every last one of them," he said.

"Hmm," I said, "Sorry I couldn't make it."

I wondered if my not being there would change our growing friendship in any way. The truth of the matter is that while I really enjoyed our friendship, the pendulum of my feelings was beginning its awkward tilt toward stronger affection. Regardless of my attempts to reel them in.

Computer Repair

I waited nervously for Jim's arrival. I had called him and asked him if he would come over and fix my computer. Its CD drive had been acting up, and it seemed like the perfect time to talk. If he were busy fixing the computer, then I might be able to bring up how I felt in a more relaxed, if not somewhat distracted manner. I didn't want to have that discussion over the phone.

He was well versed in computer repair and showed up

with all the tools necessary to work on my computer. He also showed up with his young son, Mikey. I showed them upstairs to where my office was. As we entered the office, Mikey caught a glimpse of my cat. The cat scampered off to the bedroom and Mikey followed.

Jim got down to work right away on my computer. I watched him unscrew the shell and take apart all the guts to my computer. I sat back trying to think of a way to introduce the subject I wanted to talk about as he fiddled with the CD-ROM unit.

"I read somewhere," I finally said, "that a caller into Customer Service complained to them that the cupholder on their computer did not want to stay extended."

"What?" he said, looking befuddled. "What cupholder?"

"You know," I smiled trying not to give away the punchline, "that thing you're working on right now. Mine has the same problem."

He laughed, then his expression became serious. "You know that's not a cupholder, right?"

It was my turn to laugh, "Yes, I know enough about computers to know that."

As he returned to inspecting the disemboweled contents of my CPU, I watched his hands as they worked. They were sure, and strong. I wanted to touch them. Caress them.

"This can't be fixed," he said after about five minutes of disconnecting, connecting, pushing, prodding, looking closely. "I'll order you a new one, it shouldn't take but a week or two. Then, I can come over and install it." He looked into my eyes. "Then, it should work just fine for you."

"Okay," I said.

He gathered his tools and jumped up. "I wonder where Mikey got off to?"

I followed him into my bedroom where Mikey was asleep on the bed, his hand resting on the cat who was cuddled up close to him.

"I better get him home," he said.

When he had installed Mikey into the car, he came back into my townhome.

We stood just inside the door looking at one another. He reached down and with his arm pulled me close. We kissed.

"I better go," he said.

As I watched him leave, I decided it was probably okay that I wasn't able to bring up what I wanted to say. He probably already knew.

Making It Exclusive

I held Jim's hand as we walked toward the entrance. This was a big night. This singles' group get-together was a sit-down presentation. By unwritten policy, when you showed up together to an event it was an announcement of your status as a couple. Baby tornadoes in my stomach churned as we walked in together. I wasn't sure what to expect.

As we walked in, I met eyes with a familiar face. It was Dean. His gaze shot quickly downward.

Jim and I sat down one row in front of him. As Jim was talking to someone else, Dean leaned forward and in a low voice said, "You break my heart."

I instantly felt the crush of a ceiling collapse onto my chest. Turning slightly toward him, "I'm sorry," was all I could think to say. It had been weeks since our date. Weeks that altered my entire perspective. Dean hadn't called me. I had briefly thought about trying to call him but did not do it. I honestly didn't know what the proper way was to handle it. Did one date constitute an understanding? And the time though a few short weeks felt like an eternity.

I turned my face forward rattled by gloom and despair. I chastised myself. I should've tried to contact him and explain. It certainly couldn't feel good to him to walk into it here. Why did romance always seem to have to hurt someone? The pain of pairing landed hard on so many people. Much of my experience was when I was on the receiving end of that situation. Now, here I was on the perpetrating end. That end hurt far worse.

Museum

Shortly after running into Dean at the presentation, Jim and I attended another club outing. We still weren't widely known as a couple, and this night probably wouldn't go far in getting the word out either, but we were both interested in visiting the art museum and decided to make an evening of it. Neither of us had been to the museum before. We walked in together and I immediately saw Anthony and waved to him.

The three of us talked briefly until Jim strode off for a few minutes. Anthony watched Jim until he was about 20 feet away, then he turned back toward me with a flinch in the right side of his face and steely eyes. "So, you're with Nelson?"

"Uhh," I said a little thrown off guard by his frankness, "Yes."

He was pensive and silent for a good 10 seconds, looking at the ground. I could feel a heaviness around me accompanied by a claustrophobic pressure. My nerves pressed inward toward my stomach. I felt a sudden urge to walk away when he looked up into my fleeing eyes. "I wanted to ask you out."

The shock of his admission left me hunting for my voice. When I finally tracked it down, it released my stunned reaction, "I . . . Anthony, I'm old enough to be your mother."

"You're not that much older than me," his speech now had a soft and hurt tone to it.

Jim arrived back in our presence at that moment. I looked from Jim to Anthony in silence.

Anthony smiled at us both and said, "I'm going to go

see if I can run into anybody else we know." And with that, he was gone.

The Next Step

It was December 23 late in the afternoon, Jim was coming down with the flu, and we were scheduled for our closing. The house we were building together, that we waited six months for, that we visited on a regular basis watching it grow from a large hole in the ground to cement and wood structure to complete outward finish to all its interior finishing touches, was ready to move into.

"Are you going to be okay?" I said after our closing was done. We had planned to move the next day. Having found movers who were willing to work on Christmas Eve, we were planning on merging our lives the next day.

"Yes," he said, "I have to be."

On move day, we both started early. Each arrived at the new house in separate moving trucks about the same time. Sometime during the late morning, Jim was visibly dragging.

I started directing my movers where to place each item. Boxes marked kitchen first, to the kitchen floor. Bathroom-marked boxes to the downstairs bathroom. I just completed directing my desk, a flip-top with three large drawers, one of the few pieces of furniture I had purchased new, to an out-of-the-way corner of the family room, when Jim approached me.

"They're never going to get done by 5:00 this way," he said, "and we have to be done on time."

He was right, of course. It was Christmas Eve day, and the movers would want to get home to their families.

"So, what's your plan?" I said.

"Let's have them place the furniture toward the back of the garage, and the boxes in front. That way we can get the stuff off the truck, and take our time settling in. Go through everything and decide what stays and what goes."

The plan he laid out made sense.

"Can we at least have them take the bed up to the master bedroom?" I said, "So we can have a place to sleep tonight." Looking at his haggard face, I added, "And you can take a rest later, if you need to."

"Tomorrow's Christmas," he said, "I can rest then." He gave me a quick little smile and walked outside.

I busied myself setting up the bed, retrieving linens from their box, and putting them in place. When I was done, I walked over to the window and looked out over the driveway. Boxes were stacked beside the truck being worked on. A worker stood at the back of that truck, both hands on a dolly. Jim was stooped over, one long arm jutting upward holding a large piece of furniture steady while the other hand supported the bottom of the dolly. Together the two of them slowly guided the precarious mess down the ramp leading to the sidewalk below.

I turned and left the room. As I reached the landing connecting the door to our bedroom with the top of the stairs, I heard Jim walk in the front door. He called to me, and I quickly walked down the stairs.

"Hey, do you think we should go get some food to feed these guys?" he said, his face flushed.

"Yes, I guess so," I said looking at my watch. It was 11:30.

"Why don't you go get a big bucket of chicken, a bunch of sides, and maybe stop by somewhere to grab a pizza too?"

"That's a lot of food," I said.

"We have two hungry crews here."

At 4:30, the movers were packing up their things. Jim paid the foreman and handed out tips. When the last person closed our front door, I said to Jim, "We made it."

Jim let out a groan. His face was pale. Sweat dotted every part of his clothing, with droplets rimming the frame of his face. "I think I'm going to go take a load off for a minute," he said as he lumbered toward the stairs.

I looked through our boxes for a glass and filled it with water. Then I rummaged through the bathroom boxes for something he could take for fever. When I reached the bedside with my offerings, he was asleep.

Jim did not wake until the next morning. With nothing but moving mess around me that evening, I decided to do some unpacking. I grabbed the desk box I had set aside to move in my car and brought it in. Pulling out a big black garbage bag, I sat down on the floor. At least I could sort the clutter and put my desk together.

Opening the box into which I'd thrown the contents of the flip-top part of the desk, I thought back over the day. Jim's selfless way of working alongside the movers in our employ. Pushing through the illness that struck his body. Putting the movers' needs in high perspective. (Each one of them had expressed genuine gratitude at the meal we laid out for them.) These memories clouded my mind, sending my own feeling of gratitude soaring.

As I looked down into the box my eyes went directly to a familiar object. It was Dante's business card. I'd kept it all these years. Hidden away in the cubbies of my desk. I picked it up to look at it. There was a pinpoint hole at the top of it where I had long ago tacked it to a wallboard. I could never bear to part with it. All those years.

I'd held onto the memory of Dante. I don't know if I hoped that something would change, or if I simply wanted to keep that memory close to my heart. But its remembrance seemed distant to me now. In its place, but no longer relevant to my life.

I pulled the garbage bag opening apart. There was no need for a tuna can bonfire. No angst to burn away. Just simple warm memories. Past flickers. A steppingstone to the present no longer needed. I let the card drop into the bag and into the past.

Moment of Change

Life is a series of choices. We make choices moment-to-moment. Each choice determines our lives going forward.

When I was about 8 or 9, my father took my brother and I to the doctor. I don't remember the reason. What I do remember is that he was very unhappy about having to do this. Usually my mother's responsibility to take care of us, on this day the duty fell on him.

We followed him from the car to the doctor's office. Leading the way, we followed about three to four steps behind him. It was a walk of a couple of blocks. My brother grew impatient a block into our walk and decided to break his boredom by giving my arm a punch.

"Ouch," I whined and turned toward him, giving him a shove, "Stop it."

In his retaliation, he pushed me forward, the force pushing me into my father from behind.

My dad turned and glared at me. "Stop fighting," he said, and turned around to resume his walk toward our destination.

As soon as my father's back was turned, my brother lunged toward me, pushing me off the sidewalk. Furious, I leaped on top of him. Before I could do anything more, I felt my father's strong grip on my arm, yanking me to my feet.

"I told you to stop fighting,' he yelled.

Tears stinging my eyes, I screamed a child's favorite mantra, "He started it."

"I don't care," my father's anger grew visibly deeper as he gave my arm one last jerk before releasing it. "You're older – you should know better. Don't touch your brother again."

As my father turned around, I rubbed my arm still stinging from the force of his grip and looked at my brother with tears brimming my eyes. He grinned back at me.

It was in that moment that I made a discovery. Echoes of pain reverberating around and through me. If I did not know it before, I knew it now. There was no love in my father for me. This was solid evidence. If he cared, he would've held my brother partly responsible. The injustice of the situation and my brother's smug response was unbearable. My choice was clear. No longer would I hope for the impossible. The best I could ever do from here on out was to avoid his anger as best I could.

Chapter 11 - Uniting the Pieces

<u>Experiencing Joy</u>

After Jim and I married, I shifted my attention to fixing the other goal in my life – improving my health. There was nothing I could do about the hormone issue, but I was determined to stop the ever-increasing frequency of migraines in my life. The headaches seemed to grow worse and worse. Not only was the number of occurrences increasing, but the severity and length of time before recovery was also increasing.

During this time, I also had strange experiences during my meditation sessions. A glorious, weightless feeling. A nothingness of joy. Like entering a world where you were not tethered to the earth by gravity. Where you could simply float anywhere you wanted. My body dissolving at its borders and expanding outward. Being spread like liquid sunshine throughout the universe. It was a state I came to look forward to, to long for. Timelessness. Bliss.

I wondered if this was the goal that yogis without migraines aspired to. If this was not the enlightenment that so many talked about. This feeling would also appear in my dreams. I had dreams of being able to jump, slow-motion like, from step to step, floating as I go, several feet at a time.

One dream stands out to me. Perched high above the earth on a giant pole-vaulting stick, I could vault without touching the ground, like the stick was simply a leg able to accomplish its mission by itself. I moved with grace throughout the most beautiful countryside. Mountains, and trees, and clouds. Vivid blues and white, predominant green all around. No fear of falling, simply gliding through an unblemished land. High above the earth.

In these two altered states I found joy. Joy like I had never experienced before. While I cherished this exponentially wonderful emotion through dreams and meditation, I wanted more. I wanted to experience it in my daily life. With the migraines' misery taking up more and more of that daily life, I grew more stubborn. I had to find a solution to their scourge on my life. Joy is a powerful motivator.

<u>Mints and Directness</u>

We were running a little late. Our destination a party hosted by one of Jim's friends. Feeling a little unsettled, I got into the passenger seat next to Jim. I could sense an uneasiness, a disquiet in his manner. Like fog it surrounded me, touched my skin, permeated my body and assaulted my heart. I sucked in a deep breath. Not the state of mind I wanted to accompany me to this party.

As we rode in silence, I pulled up memories of the minutes, hours before this moment. Nothing unusual surfaced. I went back further, days. Maybe if I could get him talking, he might spill what was going on.

I turned to look at him, my mouth opening to start that conversation. At the very moment I did, he looked at me, pulling a box of mints from his front pocket. His arm, mints in hand, extended toward me.

"Here, you need a mint," he said.

My sensitivities flared. "What?" I said, a distinct edge to my voice.

"Have a mint," he smiled, "Your breath in bad."

There it was again. Ever since the swan-killer sent her not-so-subtle hint my direction twenty years earlier, I had tried unsuccessfully to find the cause of the halitosis demon. Seeking out and following any advice I could find. Approaching doctors whose predictable reply was always, "Go see your dentist." Keeping my mouth as far away from people as I could, I couldn't hide it from him.

After staring at his earnest eyes for a deafening two

seconds, I snatched the mint container from his hand. Gobbling them, one after another. I bristled to the hurt encircling me. I'd tried this pseudo-solution of oral hygiene so many times before to cover up the smell. Its lack of effectiveness so evident in the flinches and deflected eyes of the person I was interacting with, their slight backward movement a harbinger of reflexive disgust.

I was happy when we finally left the party. It was exhausting trying to avoid people without appearing rude, keeping to myself while avoiding eye contact. Adding an extra layer of subconscious jitters to the anxiety of party-going.

Worst Headache Ever

The first hints of daylight pierced their way through the closed slats of our bedroom shades. Laying on my right side, I brought a cautious hand to my forehead and through slightly spread fingers looked at the clock. It was around 6:00 in the morning. Cupping my hand over my eyebrow, I slowly opened my left eye a nano-sliver. Just enough to pull myself out of sleep.

My right eye caressed a small tear between its duct and the pillow cover. An irritant wetness that often accompanied the pain segment perpetrated by the fiend migraine. The thud of tiny nerve endings pushing with all their might against the side of my head. Causing my tear ducts on, usually one, occasionally both sides to over-react. I tried to focus on the delicate whisper-tickle of the drop against the corner of my eyelid in hopes of distracting my mind from the pain. I got little response, castrating my hope.

The day was gray. Clouds allowed only a dusky stream of light between the side of the window and the edge of the shades. The yellowish-brown illuminating small flecks of dust floating carelessly in the air. This normally inconsequential light slapping my eyes, sending waves of turbulence down my esophagus. The left side of my head seemed to explode. My stomach wound in circles. I closed my eye to minimize and retract what I could from the trauma of the previous moment. The sun's assault on migraine-sensitive eyes.

The conversation I had with my doctor only two days before thundered through my recollection, proclaiming its foreboding.

"How much coffee are you drinking a day?"

"None," I answered honestly, "I don't like coffee."

Her penetrating eye caught mine. Her brow arching down, making that eye squint ever so slightly. I responsively looked away. "I swear. I don't like coffee."

"Other forms of caffeine? Soda . . . ?"

A few years earlier I'd begun drinking hot tea to ward off the inevitable headache that began at mid-morning. This ritual had become a daily part of my routine. *Harmless*, I told myself. *I need it for survival.* If I couldn't work, I would end up on the street, not able to pay my rent. After all, in the 80s, the doctors were the ones who started me on caffeine. In pill form, a combination of ergotamine and caffeine. Cruelly, like turning off a faucet, they had all at once dropped me from the medicine cold turkey.

"Tea." I struck the word like a 12th hour confession.

"You need to get off the caffeine. No more tea."

I swallowed hard. "None? But I love tea." Alcohol I could understand. It possessed evil, body harming components. I'd chosen on my own to stop poisoning myself with it. But tea. Tea was harmless, natural. And it comforted me, lifting the mood as well as the approaching pain.

"Drink herbal. It has no caffeine."

"What about decaf?" I really did like the taste of tea. Real tea. I didn't want to give it up.

"No. Just stop." She wasn't budging.

"Okay," I said. It being true I was committed to the enjoyment and taste of tea, but I was more committed to healing.

Her face softened. She took a visible breath. "You need to be prepared. When you get off caffeine, you'll experience the worst headache of your life."

So, here it was, just exactly as she warned.

I heard a soft movement and opened my eyes to a squint. Our cat, a juvenile feline at the time, stood on his hind legs. His paws rested gently on the edge of the bed momentarily. He eyed me curiously, head cocking slightly to the side, then lifted a paw and placed it near my eye on the side of my head. I knew what was coming next, "No," I said as he started tapping the side of my head.

I pushed him away as best I could without moving the rest of my body. Movement caused the nausea to increase. "I can't feed you right now, please just go away."

Undaunted, he returned his paws to the bed and reached out again. "No, I said, go away." Guilt splattered my already pounding head, but I continued with my push away a second time, "You're okay. You won't starve to death."

I, on the other hand, was not so sure of my own fate. Death by migraine. In my pain-addled brain, it sounded plausible. Even desirable.

He stared at me quizzically. I didn't want to fight with him. I had no strength. Typically more persistent, he turned and walked slowly out the door. I wondered for a moment if animals had a sense about human illness. I'd heard that somewhere before. I was thankful for his decision to leave me alone.

I could feel the nausea flutters working their way to my stomach and I took a deep breath. I needed to go back to sleep. It was a Saturday and Jim was away on business. *Sleep*, I prayed, I had to sleep. It was my only balm, my only escape.

I drifted into a restless sleep. Waking I looked at the clock. It was two hours later and the headache had progressed to unbearable. It was going to be a long day. *This is what you get for self-medicating*, I scolded myself. I tried to go back to sleep.

The clock, with its heavy tick, drew seconds on my internal time wall. Large, anomalous, obese seconds. The sound vibrating a crescendo of pain on the compromised side of my head.

Degree by degree I felt the migraine advancing. With each degree, my stomach got more and more upset. I knew that at any movement it would send me running for the toilet.

I sighed deeply. Tried to take slow, deep breaths. My stomach lurched. I knew vomit was inevitable. I jumped up and ran to the toilet. The urge of my stomach outweighing the pain in my head.

I experienced a brief period of stomach relief after vomiting. Enough to get me back to bed before it began its ascent again. This sick-to-my-stomach cycle continued about every 20 minutes.

About 10:30, I had returned to my bed after yet another round, slumped into the fetal position and pulled the covers up around me. I lay there trying again to go back to sleep. The phone rang.

The phone was in the foyer just outside the bedroom door. I tried to ignore it, the sound as deafening as a sonic boom. The volcanic eruption of our answering machine turning on reverberated in my head and made my stomach stagger. "Hi," I heard my mother's voice, "I, well I, just had this feeling that something was wrong. Are you okay?" Silence followed with only the sound, deafening as well, of her hand rubbing against the receiver. "Call me, okay?"

Great, I thought, now I must try to get to the phone. I knew when my mother got one of those feelings, she couldn't, wouldn't let it go. I couldn't blame her. I'd had experiences like that and had even done the same "call me" routine to her. But the phone was a journey of a thousand miles. The propulsion that gave me strength to get to the toilet a mere ten feet away did not work for the phone twice that distance. She would have to wait until the headache subsided somewhat.

Throughout the rest of the morning, I alternated between bed and bathroom. All the while my thoughts went to my mother. I had to call her. She would be getting beside herself with worry by now. I forced my best motivational speech. *Get up! Get UP! Go now.* My will would not cooperate. Finally, I overcame and pushed myself up. I realized my mistake as my stomach condemned my desire.

While I was in the bathroom, I heard the phone ring again. "I am starting to get really worried," I heard my mother say on the answering machine. "Please call me." I could hear a pitch of panic slide its way into her voice.

I'm coming Mom. Just give me a minute. I knew I was lying to myself. So insurmountable was that single step in the journey of a thousand miles.

Throughout the afternoon I continued my pattern. The vomit had long ago turned into dry heaves. I'd grown progressively weaker, and I was beginning to worry about dehydration.

I willed the menace to leave. A mantra of self-talk followed. *I am healthy and well. I am healthy and well. I am healthy and well.* I prayed. I begged. I cursed. The minutes droned on.

About 4:00ish, the dry heaves produced little flecks of blood. A new wrinkle to the situation.

Shortly after, the phone rang again. *I'm sorry Mom, I just can't get to the phone.*

"I'm worried," my mother's voice was in the form of a command now, "I called the Nelsons. If you don't pick up the phone now, they're going to c-c-come check on you."

The falter in her voice spurred on my motivation but did not excite my feet.

Great, now I'll have my in-laws upset. My parents lived thirty-five miles from us. Jim's parents five minutes from us.

My mother had to be over the edge of desperate to call them. I slid back into bed defeated.

Some incomprehensible time later, I heard a key jingling the downstairs doorknob followed by slow but methodical stair climbing. They walked into the bedroom. My eyes grew wet with pain, relief, sorrow, surrender. My emotions burst their confines, "I'm throwing up blood," I said.

The dam I tried so hard to suppress gave way. And the tears spilled like a waterfall.

My mother-in-law, intimately familiar with migraine through one of her sisters, looked squarely at me and said, "We're taking you to the clinic."

I had always prided myself on the fact that I never went to the Emergency Room for a migraine. I knew all I had to do was shut myself off from light and sound, go to bed, and eventually the headache, no matter how dismal, would go away. Going to the E.R. only meant giving me powerful drugs that were addictive and hard on my body. I didn't need that. Over the years, I'd known many people who had to resort to this kind of help. But I refused to let some medical record worker who knew nothing of my struggles sit in her comfy office and pronounce me a drug addict. The Cecilia-syndrome.

When we got to my HMO, my mother-in-law insisted they bring a wheelchair out for me. I must really be a mess, I thought. But I was too weak to argue.

While waiting to see the doctor on-call that day, the headache started to subside little-by-little, the nausea too. I sat in my wheelchair with uncontrolled tears dripping down the sides of my face. My mother-in-law went to find a phone to call my mother. I thanked God for all of them. My parents. Jim's parents. Doctors, nurses, medical staff. The people who made wheelchairs.

After waiting what seemed an eternity, I finally got into see the doctor.

"You've stopped caffeine?" the on-call doctor was

reading the notes placed there by my regular doctor two days' prior.

"Yes."

"How is your headache now?"

"Better," I said, honestly. "It's going away, but I'm concerned. There were little flecks of blood coming up."

"That's from the strain of vomiting. That won't last." Her eyes grew soft, and her voice became softer. "You're through the worst now. You can go home."

The Challenge

Physical weakness always follows a migraine. Pain zaps energy from the body most efficiently. In the exhaustion of the following day, I contemplated surviving. Through the din of fuzzy logic emerged a burning sense of injustice. The anger forcing its way through my mental fog.

First, I truly enjoyed having my morning cup of tea. I knew all kinds of people who enjoyed one, two, three cups of coffee with no ill side effects. Why was it I could not enjoy my one cup of tea a day? A simple request I thought. But I was no longer touching the stuff. Instead, I decided, I would be searching for a non-caffeinated alternative.

Second, and more disturbing than the simple matter of giving up tea, I was losing my life. In little bits, a day or two at a time. Piece by piece I was spending larger and larger chunks of it in nonproductive, non-life-enjoying activities. Like experiencing severe pain, nausea with upset stomach and illness. The domino effect was that I was beginning to worry about the amount of time I had to take (it was not my choice) away from work. I was sure no employer would put up with that for very long.

The migraine battlefield surrounded me. The enemy stalking toward me. Slowly, steadily. Pinning me in with no escape. The breath-stealing torment chiding me to surrender only made me dig my heels in deeper. I wasn't going to go down without a fight.

Jim once said to me that he thought my symptoms detrimental enough that I could probably get a disability from the government. I refused to succumb to that idea so long as I had a fighting chance of making things better. If I gave into the menace, I would be admitting defeat. The thought made me angrier and more determined. I decided to take up the challenge. If the migraines were going to defeat me, they'd have to work for their victory.

Fourth Angel

There it was again. I had had one of my vague inclinations that I would find a jewel, and that instinct led me to one of my favorite online bookstores. What popped up was *Heal Your Headache, The 1-2-3 Program*, by David Buchholz, M.D. I didn't often question my instinct, but this book seemed to me like just another *I've got the answer, it's just so simple, why can't you people with headaches get with the program* book. I'd been through so many times before.

While high sensitivity was becoming a part of me that I could accept, the headaches I had remained a problem I wanted solved. I was always on the lookout for new information, new breakthroughs, new home remedies. The rise of the Internet made finding the latest information easier, even if it did make it tougher to find credible information. Other changes too were happening. The medical community had, slowly at first, but with the velocity of a boulder falling down a mountain, increased its interest and legitimization of migraine as a real health ailment. With the application of validity, more and more doctors took migraine seriously. And, therefore, took me more seriously.

One such doctor, it appeared was the one who wrote this book. Even though I had spied the book some months before and had tried to ignore it, through providence or good marketing, it kept returning to my attention. I had to look at it again. Could this be yet another angel? You can't have too many of them in your life. It had been over ten years since my last *angelic* encounter. If I refused an angel coming with help for the headaches, I didn't deserve to find relief. It probably would be one more dead end, but I didn't want to turn it away if it wasn't.

Okay, so what's one more book? I thought, and flippantly punched the buttons needed to make my purchase. *I'll read it and toss it aside when I find its message is like the thousand other books I've read. Maybe then, it will leave me alone.*

Revelation

"I know when you're going to have a migraine." The proclamation caught me by surprise. We were sitting in bed, winding down from a normal day. I had pulled my book out and opened it, ready to begin reading when Jim's words hit my eardrums with supernatural force.

Stunned, I snapped my head in his direction. He couldn't have gotten my attention faster with any other statement. Jim wasn't looking at me. Instead, his head was down, eyes fixed on the book in front of him.

"What? You know when I'm coming down with a headache?" For years I had slowly gathered insight on when I could expect a headache. But it was a feeling. A sense. Internal. Also, I could pinpoint some physical sensations. Like a certain ill feeling in my stomach. And what I considered an odd one, getting the munchies immediately preceding. But all of these were internal to me. I didn't share them, even with Jim. How could he know when a migraine was going to happen to me?

"Yes, I do."

"How?" Agitated amazement flared from inside me. Impatience carried my upper body toward him.

He hesitated, then slowly brought his eyes up to mine. "Your breath smells bad."

There it was. My old nemesis. The bad breath phenomenon that I could never explain. That I could never diagnose. That I could get no doctor to take seriously. That I could never treat because I could never pin it down. A decades-old frustration. Curiosity mixed with exasperation and anger all rushed into my mind. I opened my mouth to speak, but nothing came out.

"Right before you get a migraine, I've noticed that your breath turns foul," he continued.

"So, it's not bad all the time? Just when I'm about to get a migraine?" I'd found my voice by this time, but it sounded weak.

"It's not bad all the time. But when it gets bad, it's offensive. Then, immediately afterward, you get a headache."

"What does it smell like?" The embarrassment of what we were talking about faded into intrigue. Over the years, I'd tried many times to smell it myself but had never been able to detect it on my own. I always had to rely on other people's reactions to me. Subtle cues like the other person backing off. Turning their head. Their mouth exposing a faint draw of disdain. Eyes refusing to meet mine.

"I don't know. Acrid. Kind of like sulphuryl."

"Tell me more," I said, my mind having finally cleared itself of the blur, was working keenly. One of the great mysteries of my life was at this moment opening in a totally unexpected moment. I had question after question I wanted to know. *When did he first notice it? How long had he known? Did it happen all the time? Were there really times when my breath was normal, not offensive?* On and on, 30 years' worth of questions came from the recesses of my mind. I looked over at Jim ready to spend the next five hours talking about this.

He was reaching for the light. "I'm tired," he said, "I'm going to bed."

As the light switched off, I watched it extinguish. Almost in slow motion, it left me in the dark. I put the bookmark back in place and set the book on the end table. Slowly I slid down and let my head touch the pillow. All the while, my mind swarming with activity. Like an old-fashioned switchboard operator, I started plugging in bits of information. Bad breath equals migraine onset. Bad breath caused by what? Headache triggers equal migraine onset. Is bad breath a trigger? Is it a symptom? Why didn't the medical community know this? All those doctors who knew I had migraine, and who I had asked about bad breath – did none of them understand the connection? Even when I inquired about each simultaneously? Surely, I am not the only migraineur with this problem. I smiled to myself. It was the observation of someone close to me who validated what I had vaguely deduced. They were connected. Now it was up to me to use that information.

But tonight, I needed my rest. I rolled over and tried to sleep.

Getting Serious

Spurred on by my discovery, or I should say, by Jim's discovery, my focus changed. The migraines were no longer a singular part of me. They were part of a whole. The whole of me. If there was a connection between my bad breath problem and my migraine problem, I had more building blocks to work with. There might be, there must be, some sort of causal relationship between them.

Again, my intuition flared. I had an overwhelming urge to go read the book I'd ordered but hadn't touched yet, the *Heal Your Headache* book. Cover to cover. It talked about the various food triggers. Not much different there. What was different was that it laid out how to apply what I knew about food triggers in such simple and straightforward steps. And it told me what to expect. It also produced one piece of new information.

This doctor/author's philosophy included his threshold theory. A genetically determined and preset level that dictated at which point a person with migraine proclivity would tip over into an attack and its accompanying symptoms. Apparently, not only did I have the proclivity, I also had a very low threshold.

My mind skittered over these thoughts without going too deeply into them. Most importantly, I finally had a blueprint to follow. The book suggested going full cold turkey. Eliminating all possible triggers for a period of however long it took, and it warned me that it could be six months until I saw results. I was willing to wait. After 30 years, six months seemed of little consequence. And I was resolved to keep my enthusiasm up.

I could feel it. I was onto something.

Migraine on a Plate

I dove into this program. The ember of that internal belief that I was onto something sparked hope. The fuel of hope made every cell in my body yearn for action. But the physical realities were more of a mountain than I realized.

My first trip to the grocery store proved an eye-opener. I started in the produce section as I always did. There I found my first forfeiture. My cart steered unwaveringly toward the tomatoes. They were a staple. Tomatoes are one of my great loves. They are in everything. Especially because I like ethnic foods like Italian and Mexican cuisine. But they are a possible trigger. No tomatoes. I pulled my hand back and forced myself to move on.

Cutting out tomatoes was like throwing out the list of foods I ate, seeing it scroll endlessly into oblivion and then chopping off everything but two inches of it. Determined, I did just that. Metaphorical scissors in hand, I was intent on cutting as much as I needed to trim from the sparse list I had left.

As I strolled down the internal aisles, I realized this was a waste of my time. Every item I picked up boasted a list of ingredients the size of *War and Peace*. I read the first few all the way through hoping for a winner. In a backwards hope to cheat. In the end, I realized I couldn't because all of these were processed foods. A no-no for my new dietary way of life. In the end, I gave up. With each aisle I strolled, with each ingredient list I read, my mood began to sink. Deeper and deeper as my acceptable foods list grew smaller and smaller.

In dairy, it grew even bleaker. Cheeses, another one of the staples of my diet, like tomatoes, were out. The only cheeses that were not listed as migraine triggers were cottage cheese, cream cheese and some American cheese (not really a cheese at all). Ricotta was questionable. Get out the scissors, my list was shrinking again.

Nuts, my favorite snack. No more. Sunflower seeds would have to replace them.

I looked at my meager fare. Meats, vegetables, a few fruits. I now knew how our early ancestors ate. At least they had never tasted modern cuisine, so they didn't know what they were missing. I tried to think more positively. It could be worse. It could be less choice. It wasn't. I had a good variety. In the name of relief, I could live with this. I hoped my family could too.

The next couple months would take sheer will power and a drive like the inevitable change of seasons to get through.

The Cuckoo Bird of Migraine Triggers

The cuckoo bird is a wily character. It is a brood parasite bird. It tricks other species by laying its egg in another bird's nest. The baby cuckoo hatches first and slowly gets rid of the other eggs. The mother bird blissfully continues to feed and raise the cuckoo baby as her own. While each of her own babies are destroyed. One very destructive ingredient I came across during my dietary change turned out to take its cue from this parasitic bird.

After three months of dietary restrictions, I was thrilled to see actual, positive results. It was the first time ever, after having taken advice on how to handle the migraines, that I ever saw results. I was thrilled. The migraines, and even the daily headaches, decreased significantly. I found I could go two, sometimes up to three weeks, without a migraine. A huge drop from an attack a week, sometimes twice in one week, routine of constant migraine.

My family and extended family loves Chinese food, and one day we decided to go out to eat. I was confident. By this time, I knew the foods to avoid by heart. I was pretty sure there was something on the menu that I could eat. Rice wasn't an issue. Vegetables were all good. I mentally ticked off all the components of my meal as acceptable non-triggers. And I enjoyed our get-together.

Barely two days later, I could feel the inevitable coming. For an entire day and the next, I was out. And it was one of the worst migraines I had ever experienced. Not toppling the caffeine withdrawal headache from years earlier but coming very close. Complete with nausea and vomiting, illness, and intense pain. I was worn out when it finally ended its run. And glad that it was over.

After a day of symptom-free happiness, I noticed the onset symptoms start anew. I was headed into another migraine. This one was worse than the original one. Lasting nearly two days, I retched and groaned my way through it, lying in darkness, and wishing for a way to sleep through it. Sleep was not to come. Having not fully recovered from the weakness of the first, this migraine took even more energy from me, leaving me exhausted. Again, when it finally ended, I celebrated its passing and started looking forward to several weeks of symptom-free living.

But it was not to be. Two days later, I started the process all over again. As I lay in bed, weak in spirit as well as physical energy, I wondered if it would ever end. And in my mind, I poured over what the possible triggers were that would compel such a migraine marathon. This last headache, thankfully, was weaker and lasted less than a night and a full day like the previous two.

When I finally emerged from this series of headaches and recovered physically and emotionally, I followed up on one of the intrusive thoughts I kept coming back to during my siege. MSG. My *1-2-3* book had suggested it as a possible trigger. It was the only possible suspicious ingredient. And, after recovering to a clearer mindset, it seemed the most obvious one.

I didn't want to give it credence. I'd investigated it before. But dismissed my wariness as overkill because I discovered that the FDA believed it to be safe. I wondered if any of the decision-makers at the FDA had ever experienced a migraine.

I jumped right into my research on MSG. What I found was incredible. MSG is an excitotoxin which means that it stimulates sensory nerves. Uh-oh, red flag number one. I already knew that my sensory nerves were already highly sensitive. It wasn't too far of a leap to find the link between excited sensory nerves and overwhelm. Dr. Elaine Aron had let me in on that little secret. Now I was leaping from overwhelmed sensory nerves to migraine. Intuitively I believed that my overwhelmed system was speaking to me -- no, more like shouting to me, of its pain by causing me pain that went straight to my head. It would follow that MSG, an agent of the bad guy, overwhelm, would cause me that worst kind of migraine. A repeating one that was sure to get my attention.

I dug further. MSG was a crafty little devil. Given a bad rap by some very intelligent people who stumbled upon this truth before me, companies who wanted to use its flavor enhancing properties in their foods were taking MSG undercover. I found an initial list of over 70 ingredients, without MSG anywhere in their names, that were either another name for it or contained some percentage of it. The worst of these was "Natural Flavor" and "Artificial Flavor." These two moles were in everything.

It seems these little cuckoo eggs would lay in disguise, usually at the end of a long ingredient list, only to hatch straight into a migraine. MSG was the cuckoo bird of migraine triggers. Planted into some innocuous nest of bona fide, say what they really are, ingredients was a hidden egg that didn't belong. And, at least for me, it was a health killer.

Back Surgery and Awakenings

I looked around the waiting room in the early morning pre-dawn. The pre-op personnel and nurses had just taken Jim back into the interior of the building that we'd travelled to on this quiet morning. He was having surgery on his back. The repairs done in a previous surgery 20-some years before this moment were giving out. New work was required.

The large windows of the facility were dark with night. The shadows of early morning sunlight still a couple hours away. Giving an air of gloom to my already anxious state. I chastised myself for the fear. We were in a hospital dedicated to the type of surgery he was having, staffed with doctors whose expertise was the finest in the state. But a heaviness had followed me since Jim began visiting with healthcare experts to gain their advice on his recurring pain.

Within me lay feelings of dread, a subtle anxiety, an apprehension toward the next coming months. An ominous overlay of despair sprinkled itself like a thin layer of skin around this body of emotions. These feelings tensing my muscles with restlessness. We were here now, and I had hoped those feelings would subside. I assured myself he was in good hands.

I tried to adjust to the waiting room chair, the back of which was too low, hitting me just above my lumbar region causing me discomfort. The cushions were lumpy in the wrong places. The physical discomfort lending delineation to my mood. There was no adjusting. This would have to do for the next few hours.

I pulled out the book I'd brought with me along with my pink highlighter and a handful of paper clips. I'd found it on my favorite online store doing a search for *fight or flight*. Quelling once again one of my internal drives to satisfy a yearning, much like the one that led me to *The Highly Sensitive Person* and *Heal Your Headache, the 1-2-3 Program*.

This volume I'd found was *The Spiritual Anatomy of Emotion, How Feelings Link the Brain, the Body, and the Sixth Sense*, by Michael A. Jawer and Marc S. Micozzi, M.D., Ph.D. I had only started getting into it. It was just starting to get interesting – the first part of the book being mostly a recap of things I already knew, with just enough new perspective to fascinate me. I was anxious to move into those areas of new insight.

I'd originally purchased the book so that I might understand better the fight or flight issues I've had all my life, but as I read that morning in the waiting room, I got a sense, a feeling of something bigger. A more encompassing answer to be found in the pages. I wondered if this was not yet another enlightenment angel, by now too many to count.

Sleep and Insight

The state that occurs between sleep and wakefulness, that mysterious time when your consciousness enters an altered state, has always been a source of wonder to me. I'd long ago discovered this state was a scarce but invaluable tool in my life.

Whether I had a question I'd asked myself before retiring, a problem that had plagued my waking moments all day, or the impetus of inspired reading, this state of mind would produce answers for me.

I longed for this altered glimpse because it put me in touch with insight that went beyond my waking state. Whether I was in touch with the all-knowing or whether I simply was accessing a part of my mind that held knowledge beyond my daily mindsight, I cannot tell you. What I do know is that I longed for this rare and intensely desirable state because it is where the more hidden revelations about myself lay waiting to be discovered.

"Mrs. Nelson," the words of a woman employee of the hospital standing close to where I sat infiltrated the words on the page before me.

"Yes," I looked up startled by the intervention into my rapt attention.

"We've taken him to Recovery," she said, "The doctor will see you in a few minutes, then you can go on up to his room. He should be there soon after that. There is a complementary luncheon outside his room where you can get something to eat."

She smiled and left.

After the process she described, which took longer than I had anticipated, I found myself standing in a small hospital room. A nurse came in to talk to me.

"He's still in Recovery," she said, "Go on out there and get some lunch." She nodded toward the open area lined with buffet foods just beyond the door.

It was nearly 2:00 pm, and my hunger was intense, but I was apprehensive that I could find anything that fit into my trigger-less diet.

I sat down and pulled out my book. As soon as I did, a couple of orderlies began pushing his bed into the room. A nurse followed.

"Hey," I said as he was wheeled by.

"Hi'ya," he said, a look of daze on his face. I walked to his bed and put a hand on his arm.

The nurse busied herself with adjusting his bed and without looking up said, "Go get something to eat. He will be pretty groggy and sleepy for a long time."

On this third admonition, I strolled out to the buffet and took an apple from a basket. When I returned, the nurse had gone, and Jim was asleep. I moved a chair closer to the window and opened my book again. As I did, an overwhelming fatigue overtook my eyes. My lids so heavy I struggled to keep them open, finally giving way to slumber.

As suddenly as I fell to sleep, my head jerked forward, and I awoke. I looked at Jim. He was still asleep.

That afternoon I sat by his bed fighting a pervasive drowsiness. I fought to stay awake so I could talk to Jim during his short periods of wakefulness. At various times, I tried to read but the drowsiness overtook me, and I'd nap in spurts. Late in the afternoon Jim told me he was so tired that he wanted to just sleep and that I should go home. As I walked from the elevator toward the exit, the fatigue I had experienced during the afternoon lifted. I didn't experience it again.

During my short naps at his bedside, I'd had snippets of insight come to me. They were far from coalescing into a revelation, but on the way home, they bounced around my head, swirling and tempting me with their hints.

When I got home, I resumed where I had left off in the book.

Evening Revelations

Into the evening and the night, I read, connections bursting into my mind like fireworks into a July 4th night. The snippets of insight from my afternoon naps began to show themselves in a fuller light.

The book theorizes that the bodymind (defined as the whole person physically, mentally, emotionally, and spiritually) operates initially on feelings. Emotions link all parts of our conscious selves and determine our thoughts and actions. Emotion determines personality.

The emotional spectrum of humanity lies between two extremes based on how we process our feelings. The crucial criteria being either thick or thin boundaries. Those individuals with thin boundaries are described in much the same terms as Dr. Elaine Aron's description of the highly sensitive person. Those of us with thin boundaries find that boundary between us and our environment more permeable. The resulting intensity of feeling is because our emotions are more direct, the energy forcefully piercing our boundaries. We experience the energy that drives others' emotions in our own bodies as that energy pushes those emotions through our permeable barrier.

Thin-boundaried people are more likely to experience certain physical ailments too. Including migraine. As well as experience phenomena like floating above the ground and ESP. Those with thin boundaries are also more sensitive to toxic substances. For instance, ammonia. As I had suspected for so long, there was a connection between my highly sensitive nature and the physical anomalies I had experienced.

One more point I had to ponder. The authors believe that whether a person is thin or thick boundaried, the determination was a combination of nurture as well as nature. My personality was not only a result of the way my body was built, but it was also in part determined by the way I grew up, what has happened in my life, including childhood experiences.

I knew I had a struggle with self-esteem. This had been a struggle I combated with Louise early in my adult life. And continued to fight every morning upon waking. Its insidious nature showing itself when my defenses lowered. A constant battle fought with awareness and assuring self-talk.

The two sides of my personality fighting a battle at

times with each other, at times against each other. I finally understood the sensitivity side with enough aplomb to feel comfortable with my knowledge of its nature. But reconciling the two in how my self-doubt interacted with my HSP character in different situations was yet a challenge that lay ahead.

Still, I had the start to a complete understanding in my grasp.

HSP Hits Home

I had longed my entire life for a more interactive relationship with my father. Most of what I knew about him came from my mother. And the education that comes with observation, trial-and-error reaction, and studying him like a subject that has no teacher or textbook.

After discovering the truth about my own thin boundaries and its correlation to being an HSP, I started to see what my father and I had in common. Rather than what separates us. His love of storytelling, music, and photography presented first. That desire to express himself creatively. This truth also made inroads to explain why he had a love/hate relationship with people. He shied away from crowds, even speaking despairingly about people in general. Yet, there were people in his life that he treasured. If you were one of the lucky few, he would warmly greet you, talk intimately with you, engage you. And underneath it all was sensitivity. Being easily hurt during certain interactions. Possibly, this was what my mother meant when she told me that I was like my father.

Our relationship had always been strained. I believed he never liked nor loved me. He took so little interest in anything to do with me, a wound that left me scarred. I viewed every man in my life through my father's eyes. The man whose love I could never win shading the interpretation of how any romantic interest might feel or not feel about me.

As a daughter, I didn't want to give up. I had to find something to grab what I could of him. He was an HSP like me. This was the commonality that I could grasp to bring us closer. Maybe.

Little Bits of Truth

Every day, day after day, we gather little bits of instruction. Raw truth. Here and there. They seep almost imperceptibly into the porous nature of our subconscious. Slowly building upon other little bits of truth. Fueling the formation of a cohesive thought. Kernels of wisdom bonding together. Like a flower bud, ready to burst into the beauty that only truth can expose.

Each little bit of truth, in its diminutiveness, walloping the perception of the world around us. Having a huge impact on how we interpret everything. The way we view our lives. Turning past beliefs into stone graves. Allowing the green grass to grow up from those graves. Moving ever closer to a more insightful way of life.

Throughout my life, I'd felt a searing sense of loneliness. Due in part to the differences in my sensual identity. Due to admonitions of "Stop being so sensitive" and "You take things too personally." Due to my own isolation in wondering what was wrong with me. All these bits of data, evidence to me of a flawed personality, ganging up on my psyche, dimming the light I so desperately wanted to shine amongst unbearable solitariness.

Having found the books that seemed written just for me pierced the darkness and disparity. It brought hope to my seclusion. Adding to that hope, I was now uncovering indications of others I knew who were HSPs also. A camaraderie of hope.

My father. Magdalena. These were family members. But down through the years I'd known others. A first clue to uncovering an HSP was a person's chosen profession. I knew that HSPs were drawn to certain interests and professions. Areas like healthcare, social work, psychology, and the creative arts. The latter major category of HSP-attracting professions being that of artists – writers, painters, sculptors, etc. Musicians fall easily into this category. Musicians like the ones I had encountered nearly twenty years prior to my learning about HSPs.

As I moved on in my life, Dante and the musicians floated gently into the ever-widening past. Objects at a distance. As I contemplated who my sensitive companions might be, the idea that Dante was also a highly sensitive person grabbed me. The incident on the plaza the day after the concert, when he appeared and just as quickly disappeared from around the corner of the building. Was it possible this was no accident? Could he have come to the plaza with the hope of seeing me again? Then, when I looked away, been hit in his sensitivity enough to instigate a flight reaction? The same kind I knew all too well when it came to romantic interests? I didn't want to succumb to the egotism of believing a man holding strong feelings for me with so little contact, but the graffiti from the music video and my own experience with falling fast and hard kept returning to me.

Others came to mind. Simon, my guy friend, who, on our first and only date, steered the conversation constantly back to me. My only explanation for this behavior was his sensitive nature guiding his actions toward making me feel good by allowing me to talk about myself. Without realizing that so much talk about myself, without a more balanced exchange, hurt not helped his cause. He might have been trying too hard. This demeanor having an opposite effect, making me feel so uncomfortable. So unlike what I typically expected. So far from the norm of calculated distancing that permeated expected first date manners.

I had always sensed something different about both

Dante and Simon. Both good, caring souls, kind and far from the arrogance of a verbal assault like, "I'd ask you out myself if you weren't so damn tall."

I knew instinctively how hard it was to be a highly sensitive woman. But culturally, some of my sensitivity was acceptable. How much harder it must be to be a man who was highly sensitive.

Until now, I had never recognized this shared trait between us when I, of all people – a fellow HSP, should have seen the underlying reasons. But I reacted just like a person with a non-HSP mindset would have reacted. With dismay. Because it didn't fit the expected. Me always trying to fit in to the world around me. I made assumptions. Assumptions that only applied to most people in the world but would never characterize an HSP. Assumptions that could hurt. Did hurt.

No more. I resolved to be more cognizant of the differences I see. Less judgmental. And I resolved to make my feelings known (like I had with Luna Moth) rather than hide them. My feelings were valid. Becoming vulnerable to the embarrassment was a much better alternative to losing opportunity. Or worse yet, hurting someone who didn't deserve to be hurt.

Chapter 12 - The Mere Sense of Living

Spill the Wine

Mr. Brooks is one of my all-time favorite heroes. He was an unlikely hero. My 8th grade Civics instructor, he resembled a super-skinny version of the long-haired leaping gnome described in thc Eric Burdon and War song *Spill the Wine*. Which was more than coincidence since we spent the entire year in his class listening to and discussing the meaning of that song.

He did not lecture at all on the different levels of government, make us memorize the Constitution or Bill of Rights, or recite dates important to the civil war. At least not in the typical sense. What we did was pick apart the words that comprised an end-of-the-hippie-era song. We tried to find the deeper meaning, whatever that was. And in the process, we discussed everything from civil rights to the draft and war in Vietnam to women's rights to drugs to esoteric and ethereal subjects. Mr. Brooks endeavored to welcome every opinion and delve in a little further in all shared ideas.

We never came to a collective opinion of what the song meant. But finding the answer was not the point. The process was the point. The collaboration. The teamwork. The acceptance of one another's ideas without judgement.

Years later, when I entered the university where I would get my undergraduate degree, I was prepared. This college put a strong emphasis on teaching critical thinking. It was a stretch for many of my fellow students. I had no trouble with the concept because I not only learned the skill of critical thinking in an 8th grade Civics class, but from that moment on I practiced it in my daily life. I learned to question everything. Every opinion. Every truth. A strength with more weight and importance than any I had gotten from any other class throughout my academic life. *Spill the Wine* became a symbol of this principle.

And that is what is so ironic. Our class was Mr. Brooks' first and last class he would teach in our school district. From the rumors, I learned that throughout the school year, he was constantly being told to stick to the curriculum. Which he did not do. Preferring instead to teach his students the skills he thought they most needed to learn. Holding fast to an internal barometer guided by love for his students. By what he knew to be best for them.

When we returned to 9th grade, he was no longer at the school. This is how the world treats people who act differently than expectations or what the community currently views as appropriate. To those whose courage and internal compass lead them to act in ways unacceptable to the mob, but that they know to be right.

We need the brave few who will stand up with a different idea. Those who are willing to trade the enmity of a different perspective for what they feel is right. Those who personally sacrifice for a greater cause. What greater purpose can there be than to make a positive impact on the world around us?

You Need to Come Home

"You need to plan a trip out here," my mother's voice was forceful on the phone. It was early evening with a chill in the late March air.

"Why?" I said. She historically used this tone of voice when she wanted to convince me. Or strong-arm me. "What's going on?"

"Your father is dying," she said in a straightforward even tone.

My father had been hospitalized a few years earlier. At that time, he was approaching 90 years old, and they sent him home within days telling my mother that he was dying. But he didn't die, and it was about two to three years later.

Four years earlier, we had moved to another state, 500 miles from the area in which I grew up. I wondered if this was another false alarm. During the few times he would get on the phone with me whenever my mother and I talked, he seemed like his normal self. And there were no hospitalizations in between.

"You've told me that before," I said.

"They've taken him to a hospice facility." Her voice took on a softer tone and faltered slightly at the end of her sentence.

"He's in hospice care?" That sounded much more serious.

"Yes," her voice returned to its former sternness. "You need to come now."

As I got off the phone, Jim studied my face and asked what was going on.

"My Dad is dying," I said, in a mix of uncertainty and anxiety.

"Then you need to go," he said.

Dad At Hospice

My mother tried to prepare me. "He doesn't look like himself." I had gotten to their home soon after the dusk settled in the horizon. We quickly took off to the hospice facility. "He's not responsive. He won't know you."

As I entered this final home for palliative care patients, I wasn't sure what to expect. But as I peered into his room for the first time, I realized that nothing could've prepared me for the way he looked. His face had no sign of interaction with his environment. Gaunt, with all signs of life missing, he lay staring at the ceiling. His mouth formed a large O, reminiscent of the famous painting, *The Scream*, by Edvard Munch. His eyes were wet slits.

My feet stuck in position as if they were glued to the floor. My eyes focused on the O. His body appeared stiff and small, so very small, underneath the white sterile hospital blanket. Arms straight and rigid next to his body. This certainly was not him. If my mother weren't there to validate his identity, I would've thought I was in the wrong room. I was sure he was nothing but a body missing its soul or in some interim state of absence. Who he was, how I knew him, was not the body that lay in the bed.

My mother didn't want to stay long, saying she had been there most of that day and was very tired. I was okay with that. The crush of incomprehensible emotion combined with travel fatigue from my nine-hour journey made me suddenly weak. As we left the room, I had to work hard to pry my eyes off this foreign body. The silent scream of what he had become still puncturing my own memory of his former self.

<u>Vigil</u>

Early the next morning my mom and I left for my father's bedside. As we settled down into seats in his room, my mother took out her book and started reading.

I looked around the room. The room illuminated the warm off-white walls and open curtains. The sun making its way through the windows like an apathetic healer. Lighting enough of its path to show the bits of dust floating aimlessly around the air.

Looking at my father, the white sheets crisp under his stiff arms. Real but unreal, like a snippet of a Madame Tussauds' sculpture. His expression unchanged from the previous day. His eyes unreleased from their obscure intention.

A trigger of a memory. Past floating into my mind, I remembered a moment 30 years before when I visited my father in the hospital. Never one to be hospitalized, the ambulance had brought him to the Emergency Room when he started vomiting blood. The result of taking too many aspirin to ease his headaches. The aspirin causing tiny little holes in his stomach that began to bleed in life-threatening strength.

Just before my visit, I'd gone to a stationery store looking for some small gift to help ease the discomfort I knew he would be feeling as he was forced to lay in a hospital bed. I decided on a small puzzle with a Get-Well message on it, this activity being one of his favorite pastimes. When I gave it to him in the hospital, with little expression he placed it on his wheeled bedside table and pushed the table aside.

On my subsequent visit, I returned to his room empty-handed. Before I got to his door, a nurse whom I'd met on my previous visit grabbed my arm and pulled me aside. "He just loves that little puzzle you gave him," she gushed. "He puts it together over and over again."

"Really?" I said. Disbelief edging the word.

"Yes," she continued, "And every time I go in there, he says, 'My daughter gave me this puzzle.'"

The puzzle that was my father. All the pieces felt like they were from separate and wholly opposite pictures. And now he lay here with all our chances to understand one another at a desperate end.

Fighting the Inevitable

The next day found us sitting in the same chairs in my dad's room as the day before. My mother took the chair furthest from his bed leaving me to sit closer to him. My mother talked silently about what seem inconsequential to me, what we would have for dinner, what I should be sure to take home with me when I left. The conversation left me ungrounded.

"Do you want to talk?" I finally said after a quiet period. "About anything?" I hoped she would want to talk about her feelings. Throughout my life it seemed like the two of them against the world. "No," she said, and we continued to sit in silence for long, mournful minutes, saying nothing. Or she would take out her book and read.

For me, the hopeless minutes passed slowly. A feeling I can only describe as regretful dread would push up in me like a balloon inflating slowly inside me. As it grew to a point where I thought it would burst, I'd fight it. Pushing it in from every side. I wanted it to deflate, not explode. It was an exhausting process. I decided that this was probably what made my mother want to read, and that the next day I would bring a book to distract me from the emotional harangue.

As the next day ground down to afternoon, my book only distracted me so long. I became more agitated. Seeing my father lying in this bed with little attention made me angry.

I got up and left the room. I walked to the nurse's station and said with too much force, "Why aren't you doing anything for him?"

There were two nurses at the station, a seated nurse with a chart in front of her and one bent over the shoulder of the first. The second one straightened up and smiled gently. "Come with me," she said.

We went into a large room, with a conference table but surrounded by homey texture. She closed the door. "Sit down."

By this time, I was fighting tears of frustration that seemed to have no restraint. Memories of my work in a hospital years earlier produced contradictions I couldn't settle. As I forced myself into a chair I said, "Shouldn't you be feeding him intravenously, or something?"

She looked across the table at me. With benevolence but the confidence of a well-rehearsed play, she began talking.

"When we are at the end of life, there are certain stages that happen to everyone." She began listing the physical characteristics I had already witnessed. I wanted to protest but found I couldn't open my mouth.

She went on, "People will review their life. They come

to terms with their actions. They look for meaning. It is their work before they let go."

"How do you know this?" I was stunned. I couldn't comprehend how anyone could know what my father was going through. He certainly couldn't communicate what was happening to him.

"We see it all the time," she said, "and we try to respect this process as necessary and vital to the experience of death."

I sat silent. The emotion I tried to contain blasting out of my eyes and down my cheeks.

"Here, let me get you one of our booklets," she said standing up and walking out of my sight.

As she exited the room, I pushed on my eyes with the heals of my hands, trying desperately to push the tears back inside. This can't be happening. I hardly knew my father. And now he was gone.

She returned empty-handed. "We seem to be all out right now," she said. Then her eyes lit up. "I gave one to your mother. Maybe she will let you read hers. I think it will help you understand a little better."

I mumbled a thank you and shuffled off down the hall.

The room looked different when I came back through the door. Nothing had changed. My mother still sat in her chair. My father still lay in the bed. But my sense of the room was different. *My father is dying.*

"They said they gave you a booklet," I said to my mother.

"Yes," she said, "Over there on the table. Take it. I don't need it."

I picked up the booklet, stiff with the newness of never being opened. Its cover was light blue in color, with a picture of a ship on the front. As I sat down to read, my mother announced she needed to get away from the room for a while. She left to take a walk around the facility's hallway. I wondered if she had a balloon inside her ready to explode.

My mother hadn't returned by the time I finished the booklet. It said much the same thing the kind nurse had already said. Looking around, the room was so bleak. I stood up and pulled my chair to my father's bed. Settling back in my chair, I leaned toward him and wrapped my fingers around his inert hand. After a few minutes, the nurse who I had spoken to walked into the room. She walked over to the other side of my father and looked at our joined hands. She hesitated while looking me in the eye, then leaned just behind his head.

In a light whisper I could barely hear she said, "Nearer toward the end, there are times when they will stop breathing, often for minutes at a time."

The physics of this astounded me. I said nothing.

She went on in a whisper quieter than previously, "It won't be long now."

As she left the room, my mother returned. I moved my chair back into place ready to resume our vigil. But my mother didn't sit. "I think it's time to go home," she said.

The End

It was only mid-afternoon, and the sun was bright as we left the hospice. On our ride home, my mother talked here and there carefully avoiding my father as the subject. I was silent. The talk in me absent. I loved my father regardless of the fact that we had little to do with one another most of my life. *Why could I never get closer to him? Why didn't I try harder to understand him?* I would never have another chance. Instead, I had clung to an insidious belief that I could do without his love. That it mattered not. What a lie I told myself.

At my parents' house, the nurse's words "It won't be long now," lay heavy on my attempts to engage with my mother. It would be tonight. Death would crystallize the collapse of any hope of authentic relationship I still clung to.

About 8:30, as we were relaxing after dinner, the phone rang. My mother got up to answer the phone, and my eyes lost their focus with the sting of wet blur. This was it. My father had passed.

Talking to the Minister

My mother and I walked into the minister's office. We were right on time for our meeting with her. She offered us her condolences and a seat. We were there to give her material for her talk at my father's funeral.

I was nervous. What would I, could I tell her about our relationship? All I could recall were the many sessions with Louise in which I poured my heart out about how he didn't love me. It was true. There was no time in my life when he told me he loved me. There was no time in my life when he and I created happy father/daughter memories. We didn't do special things. He barely acknowledged me in the family. In response, I rejected him as unimportant to me. This was not the sort of thing you admitted to at the time of death.

As I suspected the minister asked us each for a special memory to share. The landscape of my mind was dry, empty. There was nothing. No show of affection between us other than my attempts as an adult to give him hugs and tell him I loved him. I couldn't tell her that as I got no reaction from him.

The silence grew as I tried to think of something to say. Dry, dry, dry. I found myself fingering the webbing between the thumb and forefinger of my right hand. The scar that emerged in the center of that part of my hand had moved up over the years and lay closer to my first finger. A former shadow of itself, it was prominent enough on my hand to remind me of how I got it.

This was it, my memory.

I took a deep breath and started my story. "My father loved animals." This was true. I never doubted his love for animals. He had no compunction for showing his animals love. We had a small dog, a chihuahua, during my later childhood years. He would carry this dog around in his arms like a baby all day long. Give her special attention. I had always felt a sort of envy toward her because I never even got close to the kind of attention she received.

"We owned several guinea pigs when I was young.," I said, continuing my story. "A male and a female. They multiplied frequently, and we had to find homes for the babies. We kept one of the male children. And he grew to adulthood."

I could tell by the look on her face that she wanted me to get to the point, so I tried to keep my telling of the story as short as possible while still giving pertinent details. "We kept them outdoors in pens in the summer. And both males escaped their pens one day."

I wanted to add background telling her that the males would chatter their teeth at one another through the pen's chicken wire walls, moving their back feet in a sort of pre-fight dance as they rocked from side-to-side. "I knew they were headed for one another and were going to fight."

If they reached each another, their fight would be brutal. It was inevitable, both wanting to establish themselves as the head of our little clan. If they began fighting, they would end up hurting each other badly. "I had to stop them. Without thinking what might happen, I reached down and grabbed the younger male so I could stop him from getting to the older one."

I paused to gather myself before going on. This story was surprisingly making me want to cry. "As I grabbed him, he reached around and bit me on the hand between my thumb and forefinger. I reacted by throwing my arm outward. The force sent the guinea pig flying, but it ripped the skin of my hand."

I had the minister's full attention now. "I ran into the half bath just inside the back door to our house."

I recalled this long-ago incident so vividly now. The

pain, giant globs of blood spotting the sidewalk into the house, my screams. "My father was sitting at the table and came to the door of the bathroom. He demanded to know what happened."

What I failed to mention was how I didn't want to tell him about the incident. My instincts and prior experience led me to believe he would blame me and not the tiny fighting critters. I hesitantly choked out any answer. "I told him the guinea pigs were fighting and one bit me."

I squeezed the tears back from my eyes. "He marched outside to the pen." I had grabbed some toilet paper and wadded it up on my bleeding hand and stood gawking out the bathroom window where I had a clear view to what happened next.

"He grabbed a milk box from the patio and threw it on the ground beside the pen. Then, he reached down with both hands, and picked up the youngest male, firmly holding its jerking head, throwing him into the milk box. Then, he did the same to the older one, throwing him back in the pen. He stood up and pointed at both saying, 'Now you stay there until you calm down'."

I wiped a tear from the corner of my eye. The minister, I was sure, could not understand the full impact of this story. And I was not about to go into any details. But to me, the force was jarring.

Why did it take so long to hit me? This memory was years ago, and for so many years its deeper meaning had eluded me. For my father to have treated any of his precious critters in such a brutal manner meant that he had more concern for what happened to me than what they might do to each other. Concern for ME. He did love me. This was proof of it. Honest, see-it-with-my-own-eyes proof.

You Know He Cried

"I didn't know," my mother said. She started talking as

we returned to the car from visiting with the minister. "I didn't know about the guinea pig incident," she said.

"You don't remember the wound on my hand," I said, showing her the scar.

"No," she said.

We got into the car and sat silent for a minute.

"You know he cried," she said.

"What?" I said, "Are you talking about Dad?" My mind switching from quiet contemplation to intense attention to what my mother was saying. I'd never seen my father cry.

"Yes," she continued, "He cried when you left for school in Texas."

"No," I said. The memory returning to me. I clearly remembered my impatience, the undefined need I had to *just get on the bus*. I remembered his agitation, his distance, his lack of eye contact. His impatience to get home. "Where? When?"

"When we were sitting in the bus station."

"No," I said again.

"Yes," she said, "He cried because you were leaving."

The Long Ride Home

Dusty flatland. Gusty winds. Sun trying to peak out of obstructive clouds. And hardly anyone on the road. The droning drive home was fertile ground for my mind's fidgeting. I fought hard to keep my focus on my driving. My father's final fate was a catalyst of what good memories I could pull together when I thought of him. Throughout my life, only the strained parts of my relationship showed themselves to me.

The warmth of the incident recalled at the funeral that were "evidence" to me of his love had waned. The two sides, positive and negative, were now fighting for dominance.

Those two sides converging on his death, I now tried unsuccessfully to square his apparent happiness with our relationship. Maybe happiness was not quite the word – acquiescence might have described it better.

He cried when I left home the first time. He cried. My mother said so. I had no reason to doubt my mother's account. But this narrative did not fit in with other memories. Like the movie-of-the-week incident that happened just years before my departure to live on my own. He never spoke a word to me, approving or disapproving my leaving. Yet, when I left the television running to do my mother's errand, he made it clear to me he didn't want me to watch the movie I had so looked forward to. Simply because he had some incomprehensible bias against leaving on for a few minutes a tv that no one was watching. The irony of his running tv bias, as well as the irony of his choice of when to interact with me and when not to, was unsettling. The biggest contradiction of them all was how he really felt about me.

Whatever it was, it was not love. This conclusion had become clear hours into my drive. The love I glimpsed must have been a mirage. An illusion.

Love and Fear

I have seen it said that the opposite of love is not hate. The opposite of love is fear. Fear is absent when you truly love. If fear is present, if it grows out of proportion, it absorbs any love there might be like emotional cancer. Fear eating away at the positive, healthy cells of the love body.

My father was a fear-filled man. Fear of so many unspoken things consumed him. That fear expressed itself in anger. The anger showing itself to me most of my life.

It was the anger that I misinterpreted. It was the anger I saw as proof of his disdain for me. This was a mistake in my perception. An object at a distance that I never truly saw close. Something I never tried to bring closer to examine. Until it was too late.

Fear, I knew all too well, was my greatest foe as a highly sensitive person. All my life I had fought to gain a foot hold on fear. It was one of the reasons I was so attracted to Jim. He exercised so much courage in facing his own fears. I asked him once if he enjoyed the times in the Air Force when he jumped out of an airplane with only a parachute that stood between him and certain death. "No," was his resolute answer, "but I had to do it."

This fear, so all-consuming in my father, was something I could empathize with him on. I knew it all too well. As a highly sensitive person, I experienced my emotions with higher intensity than most people did. While that distinction gave me the ability to climb to higher heights with positive emotions, its counterpart was an experience of deeper lows. The more negative emotions. Fear, I realized, was at the top (or very bottom depending how you look at it) of my own personal emotional scale.

The fear for him must have been even more debilitating. Unlike me he chose to ignore its significance. My driving needs to understand the undefined fears in life led me to greater insights into my own makeup. His lack of understanding dominated his outlook, pushing his relationship with his daughter out to where it could never develop. All that was left was sadness and grief over what would never be.

I had to accept what was impossible for him to confront. He was human. He was highly sensitive. Instead of using that sensitivity to improve the quality of his life, he simply didn't acknowledge it. It was his way of coping. I couldn't agree with his way of coping, but I also could not condemn his decision. It was his choice.

Any remaining animosity in me toward him melted with this series of thoughts.

If I am like my father in any way, I concluded, then this is how I prefer to think that I am. The music-loving part. The creative part. The sensitive part. Those things we shared. He allowed the fear in him to grow out of control. I stubbornly fought it at every turn. If it was going to win its battle in me, it would have to put up the fight of its life.

Watermelon Vines and the Neurodivergent

Neurodiversity is a relatively new line of thought that acknowledges that human minds function differently in different groups of people. Many diverse groups of people fall into this category including those with highly sensitive brains. While it's not practical to examine this subject here, it is important to realize that differences are very real and are just now being researched and understood.

Being neurodivergent is not a brain disorder. It is simply a difference. A difference that the world must come to understand so that we can all live together with full acceptance of one another.

In my mother's flower garden, under the kitchen window, grew a host of plant life. Grape hyacinths, columbines, and a couple of rose bushes. These flowering plants, though different, all blended with one another in perfect harmony. Each having its own function.

What seemed to throw the world of that garden out of kilter was one lone watermelon vine. It's appearance and function a seeming aberration. But it, too, belonged. It had purpose and beauty. It contributed to the overall essence of its home. It simply looked different. Its neurocognitive functioning simply a contrast to what was expected.

But if you look closer at each grape hyacinth, at each columbine, at each rose, you'll see differences too. No one is like the other in its group. We are all unique, and that's what makes us special.

Acceptance of differences we don't understand. This is key to love and life. And the courage to take a stand for it. Like in Mr. Brooks' Civics class.

Normal People Frighten Me No More

I walked into the entrance to the grocery store. Looking left, as is my usual custom, I compulsively turned toward the tangle of carts. Wrestling a cart from the knotted lines of duplicate carts was a woman whose tee-shirt sported the words *Normal People Frighten Me*. I had to smile.

Normal people used to frighten me because I couldn't be one. It took decades for me to learn that it was an impossible goal. Because there is no normal.

We comprehend life through our senses, through those biochemicals, through that nervous system. Through all that is unique in our bodies, we see the world differently. And we act differently because of those idiosyncrasies and differences in bodily function. I see now that this is how it is intended to be. We must have a unique experience, a unique life, so that we can fulfill our unique place in the world. We must express ourselves uncommonly.

Relationship is at the core of this uniqueness. We are all different. But we must celebrate that because that is how we learn from one another and how we grow. As an HSP, I have an advantage. It's not easy. It's a daily struggle. Every day I must remind myself that to love is to conquer fear. It is to employ the empathy I have been richly blessed with and to understand and accept what is misunderstood. And it is vital to pull the strength and courage from within to stand up to those who try to snub the people we do not understand. Because if we don't, we ostracize ourselves. There is no such thing as normal.

Emily Dickinson was right when she said, "Find ecstasy in life; the mere sense of living is joy enough." To find your ecstasy, you must allow your senses to expose everything they want to teach you. How to love. How to make mistakes. How to forgive yourself and others. How to grow in each little moment of life. This is where true joy is found.

